"Sydney March brings to her argument the same passionate commitment she brings to patient care, with the added conviction of her Catholic faith. This book is an argument for the possibility that suffering can be endured and perhaps redemptive; her argument will have the most meaning for the committed Catholic believer. Though I do not share the religious belief, as a physician I recognize and appreciate the commonality we share in seeing the patient and the human as a spiritual whole. For the Catholic believer this thesis will be reassuring and instructive; for all others it will provide a clear insight into the strength that the Catholic provider can draw from a detailed analysis of the faith in attending to the sick, which in the end is our common human goal."

– Warren Kearney, M.D. C.M. HEC-C
ASBH Certified Health Care Ethics Consultant

"This significant work provides guidance for both the health care professional, and those they serve, to enable the sufferer to persevere and flourish. 'Suffering well' involves truth concerning the transcendent needs of the human person, so that moral and effective choices can be made, while trusting in God's providential care."

– Dr. Marie T. Hilliard, MS, MA, JCL, PhD, RN
Senior Fellow, The National Catholic Bioethics Center

"Sydney March explores the nature of suffering and its role in the Christian moral life with insight and sensitivity in this lovely book. Her enlightening reflections will be of value to all who recognize the need to 'suffer well' as we sojourn in this valley of tears."

– Dr. Christopher Tollefsen
Professor of Philosophy, University of South Carolina

"Understanding suffering is vitally important in today's world that so often seeks to escape suffering and finds it meaningless. This short treatise on suffering beautifully expounds on the redemptive and salvific meaning that suffering can beget. This book balances an understanding of the philosophical meaning of suffering with its existential reality, addressing the sufferer with compassion. It also reveals how each of us, in our own suffering, can be encouraged by the example of Jesus Christ, who willfully accepted suffering for the sake of others. For healthcare professionals in particular, we are not only called to alleviate what suffering we can, but also to genuinely accompany the sufferer, and, in some sense, to enter into their suffering. I trust this work will allow each reader to become a beacon of hope to a suffering world."

– Lisa Gilbert, MD, MA (Ethics), FAAFP
Family Physician

Freedom and Truth in Suffering

A Moral and Theological Approach for Humanity

Sydney Michelle Therese March,
BA (Theology), BSN, MS (Bioethics),
MA (Moral Theology), RN, PHN

En Route Books and Media, LLC
Saint Louis, MO

Make the time

En Route Books and Media, LLC
5705 Rhodes Avenue
St. Louis, MO 63109

Contact us at **contactus@enroutebooksandmedia.com**

Cover Credit: Sydney Michelle Therese March

Copyright 2024 Sydney Michelle Therese March

ISBN-13: 979-8-88870-218-5
Library of Congress Control Number: 2024945959

Nihil Obstat
Reverend Steven J. McMichael, OFM Conv., S.T.D.
Censor librorum deputatis

Imprimatur
Most Reverend Bernard A. Hebda
Archbishop of Saint Paul and Minneapolis
September 20, 2024

All rights reserved. No part of this book may be reproduced, stored in a retrieval system, or transmitted in any form, or by any means, electronic, mechanical, photocopying, or otherwise, without the prior written permission of the author.

Dicitur Fidei

I submit the following to the judgment of the Holy See, with great love and affection for Holy Mother Church. Whatever error is present is mine. Whatever is truth is an inspiration from the Holy Spirit. Ad majorem Dei gloriam et Beata Mater!

About the Cover

Source:

The front and back cover include a collage of photos of creation taken by the author. The boat and lilies were created by hand. The hand is a live shot against the collage, with details added to enhance the universal message.

Symbolism:

The white lily is often considered the universal symbol of joy, peace, and hope. The red "dots" were added to represent the blood that is often associated with pain and suffering. Together, the message becomes apparent that we can unexpectedly find hope, peace, and joy as we find purpose by rising above our painful circumstances. For the Christian, the lily not only represents peace, joy, and hope, but it is also a symbol of our Lord's mother—the Blessed Mother, who can help intercede for us through prayer and maternal petition on our journey of surrender. The boat is the boat of love in the quote from St. John of the Cross: "And I saw a river over which every soul must pass to reach the Kingdom of Heaven, and the name of that river was suffering … and then I saw a boat which carried souls across the river, and the name of that boat was Love." The waters: Rough waters, peaceful waters, and vast ocean waters are captured. These waters are the waters of suffering - vast, rough, but turn peaceful once purpose is found and surrender takes place. The location of the peaceful waters on the cover is higher than the rough waters because it is the internal transcendence that results from rising above one's rough circumstances. The sunset sky: the sun must set to rise again. The hand: for those who suffer, the position of the hand is open in surrender; open in reaching out to the other for help; the red markings are wounds that suffering afflicts us with; the brown markings are the chains or thorns of our suffering that can often make us feel enslaved. For those in the medical field: it is our hand that takes on their suffering in various ways through our care and compassion and carries them through their journey; both markings are the wounds of suffering inflicted on us in this process, prompting our need to surrender and remind ourselves of the dignity and importance of our role in helping our patient's find healing, and ultimately peace, hope, and joy. For the Christian: the hand is the wounded hand of Christ, enveloped with His crown of thorns, Who takes on all our sufferings, and cradles us in His love, guiding us on whatever journey is before us, and has the power to transform our sufferings for the salvation of others and ourselves by our offering, resulting in a more profound peace, hope, and joy.

Dedication Page

To all my patients in the past, present, and future, and all those who experience suffering – may these pages, inspired by you and written in humility, bring you eternal hope and comfort!

Acknowledgments

In gratitude to the One Who alone can provide peace and hope amid suffering.

∞

Secondarily, to the many who have played such an impactful role in the writing and inspiration of this thesis:

*Dear friend, Father John Paul Erickson;
My husband, Michael March;
My parents: Bob & Kathy Whitmyer;
My sisters: Mrs. Kellie Matack,
Mrs. Steffani Jacobs, and Mrs. Emily Vesely;
My patients & colleagues for their witness
and inspiring strength;
Dr. Marianne Siegmund (thesis director) &
Dr. Hermann Frieboes (thesis reader) for their time
and talent!*

Table of Contents

Dicitur Fidei i
About the Cover iii
Dedication Page...v
Acknowledgments.. vii
Epigraph xi

Introduction...1
Chapter One: Freedom, Choice, and Moral Action........13
Chapter Two: Truth..25
Chapter Three: How Freedom, Choice, and Moral
    Action Relate to Truth..35
Chapter 4: On Human Suffering and a Call to the
    Healthcare Professional...51
Chapter 5: How to Suffer Well – How Suffering & Truth
    Relate to Freedom, Choice, and Moral Action & an
    Encouragement to those Suffering............................63
Chapter 6: Redemptive Suffering, Inspiration, and Joyful
    Triumph 75
Conclusion: *"Talitha koum"* 93
Bibliography.. 101

Epigraph

Lacrimae Rerum
-Virgil's "The Aeneid"

*"'Oh, Achates,' / he cried, 'is there anywhere,
any place on earth / not filled with our ordeals? …
even here, the world is
a world of tears / and the burdens of mortality
touch the heart …
My comrades, hardly strangers to pain
before now, / we all have weathered
worse. Some god will grant us / an end
to this as well.'"*

∞

'Ode to a Nightengale'
-John Keats

*My heart aches, and a drowsy numbness pains
My sense, as though of hemlock I had drunk,*

Or emptied some dull opiate to the drains
One minute past, and Lethe-wards had sunk:
'Tis not through envy of thy happy lot,
But being too happy in thine happiness,—
That thou, light-winged Dryad of the trees
In some melodious plot
Of beechen green, and shadows numberless,
Singest of summer in full-throated ease.

O, for a draught of vintage! that hath been
Cool'd a long age in the deep-delved earth,
Tasting of Flora and the country green,
Dance, and Provençal song, and sunburnt mirth!
O for a beaker full of the warm South,
Full of the true, the blushful Hippocrene,
With beaded bubbles winking at the brim,
And purple-stained mouth;
That I might drink, and leave the world unseen,
And with thee fade away into the forest dim:

Fade far away, dissolve, and quite forget
What thou among the leaves hast never known,
The weariness, the fever, and the fret
Here, where men sit and hear each other groan;

Epigraph

Where palsy shakes a few, sad, last gray hairs,
Where youth grows pale, and spectre-thin, and dies;
Where but to think is to be full of sorrow
And leaden-eyed despairs,
Where Beauty cannot keep her lustrous eyes,
Or new Love pine at them beyond to-morrow.

Away! away! for I will fly to thee,
Not charioted by Bacchus and his pards,
But on the viewless wings of Poesy,
Though the dull brain perplexes and retards:
Already with thee! tender is the night,
And haply the Queen-Moon is on her throne,
Cluster'd around by all her starry Fays;
But here there is no light,
Save what from heaven is with the breezes blown
Through verdurous glooms and winding mossy ways.

I cannot see what flowers are at my feet,
Nor what soft incense hangs upon the boughs,
But, in embalmed darkness, guess each sweet
Wherewith the seasonable month endows

The grass, the thicket, and the fruit-tree wild;
White hawthorn, and the pastoral eglantine;
Fast fading violets cover'd up in leaves;
And mid-May's eldest child,
The coming musk-rose, full of dewy wine,
The murmurous haunt of flies on summer eves.

Darkling I listen; and, for many a time
I have been half in love with easeful Death,
Call'd him soft names in many a mused rhyme,
To take into the air my quiet breath;
Now more than ever seems it rich to die,
To cease upon the midnight with no pain,
While thou art pouring forth thy soul abroad
In such an ecstasy!
Still wouldst thou sing, and I have ears in vain—
To thy high requiem become a sod.

Thou wast not born for death, immortal Bird!
No hungry generations tread thee down;
The voice I hear this passing night was heard
In ancient days by emperor and clown:
Perhaps the self-same song that found a path

Epigraph

Through the sad heart of Ruth, when, sick for home,
She stood in tears amid the alien corn;
The same that oft-times hath
Charm'd magic casements, opening on the foam
Of perilous seas, in faery lands forlorn.

Forlorn! the very word is like a bell
To toll me back from thee to my sole self!
Adieu! the fancy cannot cheat so well
As she is fam'd to do, deceiving elf.
Adieu! adieu! thy plaintive anthem fades
Past the near meadows, over the still stream,
Up the hill-side; and now 'tis buried deep
In the next valley-glades:
Was it a vision, or a waking dream?
Fled is that music:—Do I wake or sleep?

Introduction

There are countless ranges of suffering that humanity experiences on various levels. To attempt to even mention them would be to try to mathematize their circumstances, which runs the risk of giving a mild or diminished impression of the often personal yet profound impact that suffering has on the human person, both individually and collectively. Yet, if the reality and experience of suffering and its profound impact are ignored, it behooves us to endure and seek clarity, resulting in a denial of a vivid reality that is experienced by all in some form. We routinely see suffering play out in any type of physical, mental, or spiritual pain that is experienced because of various natural events, maleficent circumstances, and even from the very choices we make. At the same time, we are charged with trying to make sense of the mysterious yet most meaningful words in all Latin poetry by the infamous Trojan hero Aeneas (see the *Epigraph* above) as the *lacrimae rerum* and expected to carry on when it seems questionably impossible. Despite the drastic circumstances that afflict humanity, we must all eventually learn to follow the path of Keats' poetic '*Ode*' on the enchanted beauty of the Nightengale's song to accept "the tears of things" in our mortality and bid them "*Adieu! Adieu!*"

There is no doubt that humanity will forever grapple with the *whys* personally and collectively within the world, leaving the doors of vulnerability open to answers and responses that are either destructive or creative and life-giving. Despite the vulnerability that results from afflictions of the body and mind when confronted with suffering, much like the resolve of the heroic Aeneas or the peaceful acceptance of the listener to the haunting sound of the Nightengale, this book challenges those who find suffering meaningless or those who choose to avoid it at all costs. The mortal feelings of enslavement, helplessness, or hopelessness can often close off the human person to an existential or metaphysical part of themselves that is often denied or ignored.[1] Instead,

---

[1] "Metaphysics' is defined by Aristotle as in the study of *being qua being*. Regarding the human person, this applies to the *soul*, which is the *form* of the body, cf. *Aristotle's Metaphysics* in *Stanford Encyclopedia of Philosophy* (8 October 2000), at https://plato.stanford.edu/entries/aristotle-metaphysics/.

it should be open to the transcendent reality of choice, albeit, not just any choice, as an alternative response in the face of suffering.

The question of freedom and truth in suffering has profound significance for the human person. While Virgil and Keats are centuries apart in their written prose of timeless and elegiac ways of expressing transcendent and universal truths on the reality of suffering and resiliency, their perceptions are the same. However, the mortal insights touch upon the mysteriously raw part of humanity to which many of us still find ourselves enslaved, grasping for meaning, understanding, avoidance, or prevention.

In modern psychology, researchers have studied concepts such as post-traumatic growth and existential positive psychology (EPP) that claim to employ a new "science of suffering" that integrates the bright and darker sides of life, including the unknown and fear of death.[2] This bidirectional approach to suffer-

---

[2] Richard Tedeschi & Lawrence Calhoun, *Trauma & Transformation: Growing in the Aftermath of Suffering*, (SAGE Publications, 1995); Paul Wong, Richard Cowden, Claude Helene Mayer, et al., "Shifting the Paradigm of

ing is "essential for creating a more complete picture of human flourishing, just as the science of pain and disease control is essential for physical health and medical science."[3] Post-traumatic growth, or transitional resiliency, revolves around the ability to choose self-transcendence when confronted with suffering. It is evidence of the power of choice and freedom when one ventures to rise above one's challenges. Experience, biological science, and the medical aspect of consent capture the reality that not only do we have free will that allows us to choose, but that these choices also result in good things when universal norms are applied and bad things when universal norms are violated; history and literature continue to

---

Positive Psychology: Toward an Existential Positive Psychology of Wellbeing," in eds Andrew Kemp and Darren Edwards, *Broadening the Scope of Wellbeing Science: Multidisciplinary and Interdisciplinary Perspectives on Human Flourishing and Wellbeing*, (London: Palgrave Macmillan, 2022), 13–27.

[3] Gokmen Arslan and Paul Wong, "Measuring Personal and Social Responsibility: An Existential Positive Psychology Approach," *Journal of Happiness and Health 2* (2021): 1–11, at *Google Scholar*, https://scholar.google.com/scholar_lookup.

affirm the overcoming of odds through choice as an intricate part of the human person.

As rational and free creatures, we can more intentionally improve and affirm ourselves through and by our free choices. This is because choice, as an act of the will, allows for a greater understanding of the relationship to suffering on the physical and metaphysical levels. Developmental psychologists even support these concepts in connection with our natural inclinations such as self-preservation, true and certain knowledge, and striving to attain happiness and live the good life, e.g., through perfection and proper flourishing.[4]

The ability to choose freely is an attribute that is often underrepresented in suffering. Authors of recent theoretical and empirical literature affirm that many view there is no choice within suffering or see it as something to avoid at all costs, resulting in an "overlook[ing] or assum[ption of] an unrealistic ver-

---

[4] Maareten Vansteenkiste, Richard Ryan, & Bart Soenens, "Basic Psychological Need Theory: Advancements, Critical Themes, and Future Directions," in *Motivation and Emotion*, Vol. 44 (21 January 2020): 1-31, at https://doi.org/10.1007/s11031-019-09818-1.

sion of human life in which suffering is nonexistent."[5] Our everyday experience and history counter this advocated notion, ultimately leaving the human person afraid, empty, and without meaning and purpose.

This book will help demonstrate to all people of goodwill the intimate connection between freedom, moral action, and truth within the taxonomy of suffering. It will also allow the one experiencing it to find purpose and value through persevering, being a witness to others who are also suffering, and cultivating actions that do not lead to despair nor choices that are counter to the dignity of the human person and natural law.

Many varying philosophies and religions have the potential to guide the human person in their actions and aid in endurance during the most significant moments of vulnerability. Which truly assists the whole human person, correlates to truth, and respects human freedom, or does it even matter? Here, the reader is humbly asked to keep an open mind, as the writer profoundly understands how philosophies and religions have been used for evil means, including

---

[5] Arslan, "Measuring," 2021.

manipulation and control. An honest look will show, however, that not only is it humanity that fails to live up to its own moral actions which result in such error and destruction, but that without a fully integrated understanding of the human person and freedom, the experience of suffering is also depersonalized and segmented in the process of their attempting to address their suffering with incomplete explanations. As a result, we are left struggling without the support of those things we need to flourish, endure, and not cause further harm through actions that diminish our moral capacity and dignity. Building from definitions of terms, this book will briefly explore why a proper understanding of the human person is essential for guidance in moral actions, perseverance, and endurance during times of suffering.

Leaving aside the human failings, including my personal contributions, I hope the reader will be able to have confidence in the reality that only the Catholic Christian faith and its moral tradition fulfill this need. Based on an authentic Christian anthropology, through a profound understanding of the human condition and belief in the inherent goodness of the human person, Catholic Christianity fulfills every human desire and yearning. It sees and protects the uniqueness of all people and respects human freedom while fully integrating the whole self. Consequently, it gives the very meaning and purpose to suffering for which the human person longs, and it provides moral principles that assist in guiding actions when confronted with suffering and the challenging questions raised in life.

More impressively, Catholic Christianity, in the face of suffering, affirms that all free actions have the potential to be salvific. It is through the grace of Jesus Christ that this is even possible. By teaching us the truth about moral action and fully revealing the Father's will, Christ invites us to pursue and live that truth through our actions and with love. Christ is the One Who "reveals the authentic meaning of freedom by living it fully in the total gift of Himself and shows us how obedience to universal and unchanging norms can respect the uniqueness and individuality of the human being without threatening our freedom and dignity.[6]

---

[6] Nicanor Pier Giorgio Austriaco, *Biomedicine & Beatitude: An Introduction to Catholic Bioethics*, (Washington, D.C.: Catholic University of America Press, 2011), 9.

While the experience of suffering is extremely personal, and we often feel unaccompanied, we are reminded that no one is ever completely alone on this journey. Because of the social and communal nature of the human person, through the examples and accompaniment of others, we can endure and have the courage to choose actions that are exercised responsibly and have an immeasurable impact on others. The perfection of these examples is ultimately displayed in the virtuous fortitude of Jesus Christ and his Blessed Mother. Their actions, also chosen freely, are crucial for not only knowing how to find meaning and endurance in suffering, but also for reminding us of their impactful and life-giving result: the most significant purpose being the effective change that opens the doors of salvation to the whole world. Imagine the natural and salvific effects, accompanied by grace, if people realized that they have the same capacity to affect themselves and others through free choices amid their daily and physical trials of life and bodily afflictions! Properly understanding the relationship to freedom, truth, and moral action within suffering, especially when revealed through Jesus Christ, united to his sacrifice, and imitated by our

Blessed Mother, provides the perfect prescription and treatment that can only be found within the Catholic Christian moral tradition and faith. Many a struggling castaway will find food for the long journey home, hope for their weariness, comfort in their affliction, inspiration to fellow castaways, and support toward the ultimate happiness for themselves and others.[7]

As a nurse and ethicist, I believe this exploration is helpful for conversion, healing, empowerment, and modern dialogue in society, healthcare, and bioethics. This exploration begins with researching the concepts of freedom, truth, and suffering and how they relate to moral action. I will provide examples for practical application, including personal and reflective encouragement directed to those who are afflicted and those who care for the afflicted. This will

---

[7] The perfect happiness that each human person ultimately desires refers to the Beatific Vision, cf *Catechism of the Catholic Church*, 2nd ed. (Washington, D.C.: United States Catholic Conference, 2000), 1027-1029, 1721; Thomas Aquinas, *Summa Theologiae Supplement, Q. 92, a.1*, trans by Fathers of the English Dominican Province, (London: Burns Oates & Washbourne Ltd, 1922), 73-80.

then be analyzed through the lens of the Catholic Christian moral tradition in a comparative theological analysis by considering human experience and actions by Jesus Christ and Mary, the Mother of God. From this research, I will demonstrate that we can choose our response to afflictions in life through our freedom. Furthermore, when combined with the power of grace and examples from our Lord and the Blessed Mother, we have the potential to find purpose, experience true freedom, persevere, and be an encouraging witness to those we encounter.

Chapter One

Freedom, Choice, and Moral Action

'Freedom' … 'choice' … and 'moral action' … while these three words are all relational, it is essential to spend brief time discussing differences, defining terms, and their relation to the human person. This exploration will also further aid the posited argument and how they relate to suffering.

'Freedom,' without any relational association, at its most basic level, is to be without constraint. This topic is well-discussed in every period of philosophy, especially Plato, Aristotle, Augustine, Aquinas, Descartes, and Kant.[1] Many scholars cannot seem to find

---

[1] Cf, Paul Guyer, "Immanuel Kant: Key Concepts - A Philosophical Introduction," edited by Will Dudley, (Acumen Publishing, 2010), 85–102; Richard Watson, "René Descartes," Encyclopedia Britannica, (4 June 2024), at https://www.britannica.com/biography/Rene-Descartes; Tim O'Keefe, "Ancient Theories of Freedom and Determinism," in The Stanford Encyclopedia of Philosophy, (Spring 2021 Edition), Edward N. Zalta (ed.), at https://plato.stanford.edu/archives/spr2021/entries/freedom-ancient/; Robert Waxman, "Five Philosophers on

a middle road between free will and determinism.[2] Philosophically, some would say that there is technically no freedom: given the world's causal nature, the only available choices are those determined by outside factors and, therefore, are not free but identical to undirected choices.[3] On the other hand, when we choose whether to watch TV or not, we are free to exercise our choice. We do not have any physical constraints preventing us at that moment, though we might feel psychological limitations if other competing values exist, such as duty towards care of possessions in 'the house needs cleaning' or duty towards providing for self in 'I have to go to work.' Some

---

Free Will: Plato, Hobbes, Hume, Leibniz, and Hegel," (2019-03-29), at https://philarchive.org/rec/PHDFPO; Aquinas citation is further within the paper.

[2] See footnote 9, as well as Hari Narayannan, "Freedom, Responsibility, and Jurisprudence," *Balkan Journal of Philosophy,* Vol. 10, Issue 1 (2018): 55, at CINAHL, https://web.p.ebscohost.com/ehost/pdfviewer/pdfviewer .

[3] Narayannan, "Freedom, Responsibility, and Jurisprudence," 55; Francesco Botturi, "Liberta e formazione morali," in *Alla Ricercar delle Parole: La Familglia e il Problema Educativo,* trans. in Google Translate, ed. G. Borgonovo, (Casale Monferrato: Piemme, 2000), 36-53.

might even say there is no real ability to choose freely, given our own deliberation between alternatives and pressing needs.[4] Nonetheless, one cannot deny that the ability to choose in and of itself still exists within the reality of deciding whether to watch TV (leaving motive aside) regardless of the circumstances. Plenty of empirical data indicate that human will is free in some capacity when applied to experience and how we organize ourselves and relate.[5] This data is evident in many areas of life: jurisprudence, prohibitions or exhortations of specific behavior, medicine, scientific research, and politics. The colloquial use is often applied in matters of consent, autonomy, and exercised rights. Undoubtedly, "[M]an is a moving principle or begetter of his actions as of children."[6]

---

[4] Din Bandu, M. Murali Mohan, Noel Anurgg Prashanth Nittala, et al., "Theories of Motivation: A Comprehensive Analysis of Human Behavior Drivers," *Acta Psychologica*, Vol. 244, (April 2024), at https://doi.org/10.1016/j.actpsy.2024.104177.

[5] Aquinas, *Summa Theologiae Ia, Q. 83, a.1*, 147-150.

[6] Aristotle, *Nicomachean Ethics 113b, Bk III, 5*, trans W.D. Ross, in *The Basic Works of Aristotle,* (New York: Random House, 1941), 972.

The ability to choose or deliberate proceeds from the will, which as the rational appetite is part of our human nature.[7] It is this aspect of freedom that is my principal focus, which is on the extended faculty of freedom in the internal and primary action taking place in the mind. Possession of reason and will entitles freedom. They are united in the ability to act or not, provided they are not affected by subconscious reflexes or compulsive addiction. In other words, the movement of freedom exists when we cross the deserted road despite the "walk" sign not being lit, signaling us to cross. While positive law associated with the previous scenario is not a point of comment, the mind has gathered external data, reasoned that it is safe, does not need a signal to declare it so, and can choose to cross. It is an action in the mind that has been deliberated, selected in the intellect, and then propelled by the will from its permission to fulfill the action of moving the body and achieving its original purpose or motive.

A few final points are offered within the context of freedom and the ability to choose. Deliberation is

---

[7] Cf, Aquinas, *Summa Theologiae I.b, Q6, a2,* 91.

the hallmark of a rational and thinking being—*persona est rationalis naturae individua substantia*—and an integrated understanding of freedom is necessary for order and self-fulfillment.[8] While this thesis previously defined freedom as being without constraint; this also does not mean that we should do whatever we want or will do even though we certainly can, barring a barrier. The problem lies in understanding freedom as pure initiative or exclusive autonomy – unfettered freedom isn't possible in a world where desires must have governance over emotions and choices. Experience shows us that we cannot always do what we want, even though we can. Positive law, other types of jurisprudence, cause and effect, and even ethics committees within hospitals and other disciplines demonstrate this notion in a limited way. Laws and norms help govern actions and allow a coexistence with exercising freedom for the good, which provides self-fulfillment and flourishing.

Contrary to some philosophical and scientific schools of thought, the human person is more than

---

[8] One can find the definition in Boethius' *Liber de Persona et Duabus Naturis*, Ch. 3.

mere biology or simply a "chemical machine" that relates all actions of every life form to reductionism, an obvious denying reality.⁹ Both experience and biology demonstrate this reality between the three levels in the hierarchy of life (vegetative, sensitive, and rational/intellective). The distinction among them results from two criteria: autonomy and superior intelligence to the nonliving world:

> In vegetative life, both the end of the imminent action and the form of that action are determined and not optional. An animal, through its cognitive and sensory life, chooses the form of its own action based on a cognitive form (i.e. feeding on grass or fleeing from a man, in the case of a rabbit). In addition to choosing the form of the activity and its execution thereof, man also choose the end of his action; the purpose for which he acts is chosen through his free, intellective life. Since it is free, this choice entails ethics. Vegetative

---

[9] Jacque Monod, *Chance and Necessity: An Essay on the Natural Philosophy of Modern Biology*, trans. A Wainhouse, (New York: Knopf, 1971), 45.

Ch. 1: Freedom, Choice, and Moral Action 19

life, sensitive life, and intellective life therefore reveal not only differences of degree but also levels of superiority.[10]

Indeed, what is needed is an integral freedom that "combines the idea of autonomy wherein one accepts one's dependence on others and on the good and an idea of choices that is fulfilled in fidelity to the freedom of others together with what attains the good of the subject."[11] Karol Wojtyla, a philosophical phenomenologist (like Edmund Husserl and Max Scheler), in *Person and Act*, demonstrates a sound relationship between choice and freedom, which culminates in moral action: "The will is not only a 'capacity of nature' but also a 'property of the person.' The moment 'I want' suggests a personal structure that includes 'I can, but I am not compelled,' an expression of fundamental freedom."[12]

---

[10] Elio Sgreccia, *Personalist Bioethics: Foundations and Applications*, (Philadelphia, PA: The National Catholic Bioethics Center, 2012), 80.

[11] Botturi, *Liberta*, 47.

[12] Miguel Acosta and Adrian Reimers, *Karol Wojtyla's Personalist Philosophy: Understanding Person & Act*,

What, then, is meant by moral action regarding the human person? By acting, an end is an intention, and in that intention or motivation, there is the value associated with it or a desire for some good for the one acting. Moral action in human choices relates to moral value:

> In particular, moral value is specific to human activities and to moral experience and denotes the quality of perfection an action or behavior insofar as it conforms to the good or to the dignity of the human person. Love of neighbor, respect for life, generosity, a spirit of sacrifice, and so forth are moral values. Values exist as an inherent appeal within the very reality of the human person, as an ideal that continually attracts the personal subject – an *ought to be* toward which to direct one's being. As such, they are the presupposition and fundamental condition for the existence of moral

---

(Washington, D.C: Catholic University of America Press, 2016), 118.

discourse, in terms of both personal action and scientific reflection.[13]

These values transcend the human person rather than result from any type of subjectivism. Furthermore, by definition, if they are subjective, then they cease to be universals or norms. Their essence stays the same, transcending time and history, but undergoes an accidental change in awareness, relation, and practical application. When one acts, one is doing so fundamentally as a moral being who operates by effectively changing things in the world. One is aware of this "otherness" in their consciousness, which is outside themselves, and in seeing a privation of a good that should be there, desires to change it for the better. Wojtyla also expounds upon the same transcendental aspect and points out that when the human person is acting, the action takes place by that person's going out of him- or herself to fulfill it: "The person is motivated by values to undertake actions ... for one must act effectively to attain what he wants. The desire for value by its very nature points to the

---

[13] Sgreccia, *Personalist Bioethics*, 164.

non-self, because the appetite is a desire for what one lacks."[14]

Moral action, however, ordered towards the good of the human person, cannot happen without an ethical foundation in the natural order of the universe. It must point to the values associated with actions meant to direct humanity toward and help it attain what all seek: happiness. Failure of this results in disunity, in a word, unhappiness and disintegration, as evident in common experience and historical evidence. In fact, if not exercised well, one's action can potentially cause and even worsen their suffering. Hence, evaluation of choices becomes important so one can learn how to act well.

In summary, freedom and choice exist within the human person by nature of the ability to reason and the existence of free will. While motive or behavior are present as determining factors, propelling the will towards a choice inclined toward some perceived good, this does not mean that freedom is non-

---

[14] Acosta and Reimers, *Karol Wojtyla*, 49.

existent. There is still the ability to refrain from a choice despite motive or behavior.[15]

Experience and the order of nature demonstrate that the human person is not purely a biological machine or one whose choices boil down to pure determinism. The metaphysical side of the human person needs emphasis in relation to the values attached to one's choices. The value in the 'goodness' or 'badness' of the action transcends one and impresses meaning upon life:

> Aquinas spoke of *ens* (being) and *bonum* (good); contemporary thinkers speak about reality (things, persons, institutions, or expressive forms such as art, technology, and religion) and values. What contemporary philosophy brings to light is the personalist element: values have meaning for man and do not exist without man. This is also evident in the vocabulary changes that have occurred in reference to man's ultimate end: antiquity spoke of *eudaimonia*, the Middle Ages spoke

---

[15] Aquinas, *Summa Theologiae Ia, Q. 83, a.1*, 147-150.

of the *beatific vision*, and contemporary language speaks of *self-realization*. Yet these perspectives are not mutually incompatible so far and nothing prevents us from adopting the new terminology, given the change in cultural sensibilities. The delicate point here is the *foundation of values*.[16]

This reality alone points to the metaphysical part of the human person that should not be dismissed.

Finally, an additional and essential element of clarification regarding these values is that they are not subjective. They do not change in essence but correspond to an objective ontological foundation that touches upon the meaning of the human person that transcends material reality. Without a structure or moral foundation, it would cease to be considered a value in and of itself, which is the importance of correspondence with universal truths. These truths are aided by the natural light of practical reason and participate in higher metaphysical realities, expounded upon in the next chapter.

---

[16] Sgreccia, *Personalist Bioethics*, 165.

Chapter Two

Truth

"'Beauty is truth, truth beauty,' that is all ye know on earth, and all ye need to know." In the words of John Keats in his *Ode on a Grecian Urn*, this incredibly profound literary statement captures the very foundation of our understanding of the world through causes and the eternal call placed within the heart of every human person: the desire to know and to know thyself. While Keats' line is only part of an explanation of truth, it touches upon the metaphysical aspect of the world that cannot all come from empiricism or mere sensation. The aesthetic is a primary avenue where this is appreciated: the beauty of a symphony, prose, or painting. In them, we grasp the order of the whole put together by individual notes, words, colors, or shapes. Together and in a certain way they form a whole composition of something much deeper about humanity, reality, and even the metaphysical. We find meaning and some form of fulfillment in them – we see value. Additionally, after enduring a challenging

situation, we can find the same experience in our various accomplishments or after persevering in that challenge. In essence, directing our actions through order or reason is where we see most fulfillment.

Reason and order are also what we seek when plagued with fundamental questions on knowledge of self and the world, including suffering. They cannot escape the continuous questioning of the human heart. Ancient writings and literary dramas in different parts of the world pour words over this journey of personal self-discovery and knowledge:

> The admonition *Know yourself* was carved on the temple porta at Delphi, as a testimony to a basic truth to be adopted as a minimal norma by those who seek to set themselves apart from the rest of creation as 'human beings,' that is as those who 'know themselves.' … These are the questions which we find … in the Veda and the Avesta; we find them in the writings of Confucius and Lao-Tze, and in the preaching of Tirthankara and Buddha; they appear in the poetry of Homer and in the tragedies of Euripides and Sophocles, as they

do in the philosophical writings of Plato and Aristotle.[1]

This vigorous pursuit of the truth, search for meaning, and appreciation of order made present in various artistic and natural realities connect to *what makes us human*, which is a property of our rational human nature. Our very nature allows us to derive from the same speculative awe and wonder of the world, universal truths, and certain elements of knowledge. As a result, this enables us to know more about ourselves and one another, to see how things are connected, to attach meaning to them, and to advance in various areas that we deem deficient.

The main function of human reason is to "direct… steps towards a truth which transcends them," making us more receptive to the eternal truths placed

---

[1] In humility, the reader is asked to be open to citations that openly touch upon humanity and its inherent goodness, such as the intellect, beauty, and transcendental vision, for which he is called to integrate through virtuous behavior; John Paul II, Encyclical Faith and Reason *Fides et ratio* (14 September 1998), §1.

within our hearts.[2] It makes the human person by nature a moral being. It also provides partial aid and guidance to human flourishing and fulfillment despite all odds, without which a lapse into meaningless and hopeless living prevails. Additionally, without reason, humanity would be left to their unnatural vices, injustices, and the merciless will of the rich and powerful. It would be proclaimed inferior and placed at the relative whim of political power:

> [Natural law] designates a fact rather than a theory ... that human reason is, in and of itself, practical and moral reason ... [that] springs forth from human nature, finding in the latter a supporting structure without which it would be external, extrinsic, repressive, and unbearable authority – indeed an unintelligible one.[3]

While not all elements of natural law, including its critiques, can be examined here, what is examined

---

[2] *Fides et ratio*, §5.

[3] Sgreccia, *Personalist Bioethics*, 165.

is its classical definition in connection with universal truths and truths that transcend the world.[4] Both in definition and identifying these connections, they stand *quod erat demonstrandum* amidst the critics who prefer the whim of the state or the worldview of positivism that sees the human person as mere physics rather than both physical and metaphysical.[5]

The human person is more than a body and chemicals randomly put together. It is one whose additional intellectual prowess includes knowledge of things or universals that expands the subjectiveness and empiricism of one's inward thinking. Clarity is essential with this topic, mainly when it is applied to the actions of the human person and seen within the context of human freedom. Such clarity is necessary to guard the powerless and vulnerable and ensure

---

[4] "Classical" means Aristotelian and Thomistic; Aquinas, *Summa Theologiae I-II, Q. 91*, 9-21.

[5] *Quod erat demonstrandum* is an Euclidian Latin phrase indicating that the argument's proof is complete. Philosophers such as Hume, Comte, and Bentham, among others, argued adamantly against natural law – cf., Philip Milton, "David Hume and the Eighteenth-Century Conception of Natural Law," *Legal Studies*, 2, no. 1 (1982): 14-33, https://doi.org/10.1111/j.1748-121X.1982.tb00278.x.

that civil laws reflect natural law rather than the frequently changing whims of the masses.

Natural law is the light of our intellect through which moral realities are accessible to us and is our rational participation in the eternal law, which is evident by the fact that there can be no cause without a First Cause that governs the universe.[6] Following the trail of causes, natural law is logically infused by the First Cause – God. This type of knowledge is accessible to all and does not require specialized degrees, a prominent place within society, or acquired riches. It has served many a legislative and legal society, especially promoted among the remarkable philosophical antiquities, and has defended human rights and dignity claims. It espouses first principles such as non-contradiction, intrinsic human goodness and worth, doing good, avoiding evil, self-preservation, finality, causation, knowledge of God, and veracity, among others.[7] It bears a desire for the complete human

---

[6] Angel Rodriguez Luno, *Etica*, (Florence: Le Monnier, 1992), 213.

[7] C.S. Lewis's *Abolition of Man* draws from diverse cultures, religions, and discourses, and expounds on eight major natural laws. Two of the eight are above, and the

good and values consistent with the supreme good or happiness of the human person. Through personal contemplation and experience, it can also arrive at other truths that are associated with first principles which deal with precepts of neighborly charity:

> With the help of sociology and ethnology, some scholars recognize them in respect for others as persons and in the prohibition of homicide, incest, and so forth, but reason must always reflect—sometimes imperfectly and with difficulty and something vacillating—and learn to find the specifications of the natural in particular situations, striving to purify social behaviors of false "natural" justifications. The necessary mediation of reason has been emphasized because, once again, there is no ethics without objective support-

---

remaining are special beneficence; duties to parents, elders, and ancestors; responsibilities to children, posterity, mercy, justice, and magnanimity. Cf. Thomas Aquinas, *Summa Theologiae, I-II, q. 18-19; II-II, q.10 a. 3; I-II, q.72.*

ing reasons and without rational refinements to one's own behavior.[8]

In a time of depersonalization, malice, and strife in the workplace and society, there is a natural need for a moral foundation that calls the human person out of himself to virtuous behavior that is integrated into personal and communal life.

Natural reason, however, can only take us so far: "the natural limitation of reason and the inconstancy of the heart often obscure and distort a person's search …life in fact can never be grounded upon doubt, uncertainty or deceit; such an existence would be threatened constantly by fear and anxiety."[9] Naturally and logically, this points to the need to evaluate why there is such a restless heart filled with fear, anxiety, and distrust of truth made evermore present in such apparent ways within the world that do not require verbal proof from psychologists or scientists. A glance at social media or the news suffices.

---

[8] Sgreccia, *Personalist Bioethics*, 166.
[9] *Fides et ratio*, §28.

In conclusion, the responses are universal when in their weakest moments, human persons experience suffering and vulnerability. All people inherently seek One Absolute that gives all their searches and questions a more profound meaning, Whose ultimate answer is not evident in data. These questions supersede whether one is rich, poor, African American, Native, Spanish, Muslim, or Asian. No one can avoid the questioning or the desire to know.

A further step, however, is necessary in this quest for answers. This further step is also the only solution that gives rise to the metaphysical, thereby integrating the human person in their moral actions in a more complete way. There is a reason why there is so much dissatisfaction and lack of fulfillment leading to bottomless searches and continued mental anguish. The solution goes beyond the finite searches of this world. The enlightenment of faith and gift of grace, addressed in the following chapter, is what is needed and brings freedom, choice, and moral action properly under the umbrella of truth.

Chapter Three

How Freedom, Choice, and Moral Action Relate to Truth

"Faith and reason are like two wings on which the human spirit rises to the contemplation of truth; and God has placed in the human heart a desire to know the truth – in a word, to know himself – so that, by knowing and loving God, men and women may also come to the fullness of truth about themselves."

– John Paul II, Fides et Ratio

Religion and faith are sensitive topics to discuss. Hesitancy to keep an open mind is understandable because many examples exist of people who espouse a particular faith but do not live it out in an integrated way. It seems to me that this disconnect is also related to a fundamental problem with moral actions being counter to truth and not acknowledging the true needs of the human person. This book answers in the affirmative, and throughout it clarifies and expounds upon what is meant by integration, dualism, truth, and the human person.

For most religions, full integration is not possible, secondary to forms of dualism and a lack of complete understanding of the human person.[1] Integration comes from the Latin word integer: "From the psychological and philosophical point of view, the word … is used to speak about the attainment and manifestation of a whole and a unit that is constituted by

---

[1] Richard Wood, "In Defense of Dualism: Competing and Complementary Frameworks" in *Religious Studies and the Sociology of Religion in Critical Research on Religion, Vol. 4(3),* (SAGE, 2016), 292-298 at ATLA: https://web.p.ebscohost.com/; Stevri Lumintang and Benyamin Intan, "Theology and Science: An Analytic-Synthetic Integration Model: Solution to the Problem of Dualism and Secularism" in *Unio in Christo, 8 No. 2,* (Oct 2022), 239-257 at ATLA: https://web.p.ebscohost.com/; Sandra Wawrytko, "Aesthetics of Attentional Networks: Chinese Harmony and Greek Dualism" in *Journal of Chinese Philosophy, 47 No. 1(2),* (2020), *12-30*; Ralph Stefan Weir, *Christian Physicalism and the Biblical Argument for Dualism* in International Journal for Philosophy of Religion *No. 91* (2022), *115-138,* at ALTLA: https://web.p.ebscohost.com/.

Ch. 3: Freedom, Choice, and Moral Action

certain complexity."[2] In order for the human person to be fully integrated, there are physical and metaphysical needs that must be met, including an integrated understanding of who we are in both the physical and metaphysical sense. This, however, is not the *dualism* of Descartes, Plato, and Spinoza, among others. Dualism is the belief that either the human person is made of a separate body and soul, or the body (evil) is constantly at odds with the soul (spiritual/good).[3] Principally, it is Jesus Christ who integrates the whole human person (mind, body, heart, and soul), including the respect of personal autonomy and freedom. His teachings are made present through His Church, biblically expounded upon by many theologians, and lived out fruitfully through the lives of the saints, especially those who have suffered. Secondarily, there is no belief in dualism.[4]

---

[2] Acosta and Reimers, *Karol Wojtyla*, 188.

[3] Wood, "In Defense of Dualism," 292-298; Lumintang, "Theology and Science," 239-257; Sandra Wawrytko, "Aesthetics," 12-30; Ralph Stefan Weir, "Christian Physicalism," 115-138.

[4] The human soul is the substantial form of a human body, and body and soul together make up one substance, also known as, a body-soul composite. It would seem that

While dualism is not the focus of this book, it is discussed to provide context for understanding the human person, and the relationship between freedom, choice, moral action, and truth as the human person exercises these operative functions. This understanding cannot be separated from human anthropology, lest it lead to disintegration. Furthermore, and with great humility, this understanding provides a fittingness for Jesus Christ through the moral and sacramental traditions of the Catholic Church that provide the truth and peace that all people genuinely seek:

> Underlying all the Church's thinking is the awareness that she is the bearer of a message which has its origin in God himself (cf. 2 Cor 4:102). The knowledge which the Church offers to man has its origin not in any speculation of her own, however, sublime, but in the

---

this is dualistic, but it is not in the sense that all things have matter and form, or what the thing is made of and the shape that gives its specific difference. This does not make things "two," but together they make up one substance, cf. Aquinas, *Summa Theologiae Ia, Q. 75-76*, 3-54.

word of God which she has received in faith (cf. Th 2:13). At the origin of our life of faith there is encounter, unique in kind, which discloses a mystery hidden for long ages (cf. 1 Cor 2:7; Rom 16:25-26) but which is now revealed: 'In his goodness and wisdom, God chose to reveal himself and to make known to us the hidden purpose of his will (cf. Eph 1:9), by which, through Christ, the Word made flesh, man has access to the Father in the Holy Spirit and comes to share in the divine nature.' This initiative is utterly gratuitous, moving from God to men and women in order to bring them to salvation. As the source of love, God desires to make himself known; and the knowledge which the human being has of God perfects all that the human mind can know of the meaning of life.[5]

There are two modes of knowledge: natural, which is human reason that includes receptivity towards the metaphysical, and knowledge beyond the

---

[5] *Fides et ratio*, §7.

natural (supernatural). While human reason can discover metaphysical elements, such as the proofs of the existence of God and knowing many of His attributes; the other source is divine faith through grace exercised and accepted in freedom, which is the knowledge that "expresses a truth based upon the very fact of God who reveals himself, a truth which is most certain since God neither deceives nor wishes to deceive."[6]

Human freedom and choice are key aspects in accepting divine faith by the human person and on behalf of God. It is not forced or coerced, nor does it take over or fight, but works within the human person, building upon the intellect and will in freedom.[7] This acceptance is an action within itself, whereby afterward, it enables the "[human person] to act in a way which realizes personal freedom to the full[est,] …for it is here that freedom reaches the certainty of

---

[6] *Fides et ratio*, §7; Aquinas, *Summa Theologiae Ia, Q. 2-11,* 19-119.

[7] Wood, "In Defense of Dualism," 292-298; Lumintang, "Theology and Science," 239-257; Sandra Wawrytko, "Aesthetics," 12-30; Ralph Stefan Weir, "Christian Physicalism," 115-138.

truth and choose to live in that truth."[8] Christian Revelation in the Catholic moral tradition enables the human person to embrace all life mysteries with an openness that respects their personal autonomy and freedom. Thus, our actions are opened to being aligned with truth; Jesus Christ is the harbor of truth that leads people to full self-realization and freedom:[9]

> It is essential, therefore, that the values chosen and pursued in one's life be true, because only true values can lead people to realize themselves fully, allowing them to be true to their nature. The truth of these values is to be found not by turning in on oneself but by opening oneself to apprehend that truth even at levels which transcend the person. This is an essential condition for us to become ourselves and to grow as mature, adult persons.[10]

If this alignment is necessary for self-realization and freedom, it is also necessary for flourishing and

---

[8] *Fides et ratio*, §13.

[9] See further below clarity on self-realization.

[10] *Fides et ratio*, §25.

happiness. They are not opposed to one another, but compatible in the sense that they work together like a flower that needs the sun and water to maintain and grow.

What is truth? The definition of truth, whose same definition is not only in Merriam-Webster's dictionary but also ascribed to by Aristotle and Aquinas, is that truth is the *adequatio intelletus et rei* – the conformity of the intellect to the thing or reality.[11] It is something that cannot be reduced or founded upon the self and is the proper object and intention of action, without which the action would not be properly effective, and may even be harmful. To act effectively implies a certain understanding of reality—a reality that does not conform, but simply is, and is present in man in a particular and special way: "The splendor of truth shines forth in the works of the Creator and, in a special way, in man, created in the image and likeness of God. Truth enlightens man's intelligence and shapes his freedom, leading him to know and

---

[11] Aquinas, *De Veritate* I at https://catholiclibrary.org/library/, I; *Merriam-Webster's Online Dictionary,* truth Archived 2009-12-29 at the Wayback Machine, 2005 at https://www.merriam-webster.com/dictionary/ truth.

love the Lord."[12] While this understanding is also an understanding of the whole or universals, it is also not solely an assembling of facts, sensory data, or raw empiricism but an understanding in which we can know things as things in and of themselves. It implies and consists in the formation by "informing" the mind.[13]

Since we can know the truth about the world or things in order to act and change effectively, we can also know the truth about the human person. It is in knowing this that we can look forward to being truly integrated and act in accordance with who we truly are and with our dignity as human persons. It is, however, not enough. Self-realization, fulfillment, flourishing, and happiness on the natural level, however, can only progress to a certain point. With the aid of grace from Revelation and the gift of faith under the Catholic Christian moral tradition, however, we are made capable of so much more, which allows us to experience a type of 'otherness' when we live out actions that call us to transcend ourselves. Concretely,

---

[12] John Paul II, The Splendor of Truth *Veritatis splendor*, (Boston, MA: Pauline Books & Media, 2003), §9.

[13] Acosta and Reimers, *Karol Wojtyla*, 68.

provided they are oriented to the truth, this is experienced in acts of love and service towards someone other than us.

On the other hand, the opposite of integration is disintegration or those acts that are not love and service, but "show an incapacity of the person for self-dominion or self-possession. It is a lack that limits one's actions ... [,therefore,] he cannot reach normality."[14] On the physical level, this is apparent in finding or experiencing ailments within the human body or mind. On the psychological level, it is experienced in natural impulses that are overrun by our unmoderated desires, such as eating too much or when our actions induce mental health unrest.[15]

---

[14] Acosta and Reimers, *Karol Wojtyla*, 190.

[15] Negative and positive choices have a significant impact on mental health in Rashid Zaman, Ahmed Hankir, Monem Jemni, "Lifestyle Factors and Mental Health" in *Psychiatry Danub 31 (Suppl 3)*, Sep 2019, 217-220 at https://pubmed.ncbi.nlm.nih.gov/31488729/; likewise to do bad or to sin is also regarded as an illness of the soul where healing is needed that also has significant impact on the psyche in Metropolitan of Nafpaktos Hierotheos, *The Science of Spiritual Medicine: Orthodox Psychotherapy*

Christian Revelation in the Catholic moral tradition also becomes more important in acknowledgment when we are unsure of how and/or when to act. It not only aligns our actions with truth, provided those actions correspond with truth and we choose to follow through with them, but it also provides an ethical framework for moral action, especially in particular circumstances. One major principle that provides direction within ethics-related disciplines in medicine, technology, business, politics, science, etc., which is discussed later, is if the human person is meant to possess and realize themselves fully, then the human person can never be used as a means to an end, as someone else's instrument, or instrumentalize themselves.[16]

The ethical framework for moral action is the traditional and Thomistic understanding of object, intention, and circumstance. This simply explains the correspondence of the mind conforming to the thing

---

in Action, (Levadia, Greece: Birth of Theotokos Monastery Pelagia, 2010), 27-29.

[16] The personalistic norm from both phenomenologist Karol Wojtyla and Immanuel Kant, upon which many medial tenants are based.

or reality and then making that reality present in the form of action; limited, practical applications are presented in later chapters. In essence, acts subject to moral analysis are either good, bad, or neutral when the object, intent, or circumstance is such, and the will freely chooses it. In order for an act to be good, all three elements must be good as a whole. Because freely chosen acts shape, mold, and affect us in a certain way, we are therein morally accountable for them. As Aquinas explains,

> A human act receives its characterization as good or bad from the end, which is the object of the interior act of the will, and from the object of the exterior act, which depends on the interior act of the will for its very characterization as moral.[17]

The object specifies the act itself—*what is being done*. It involves the behavior of the proximate end in a deliberate decision. The intention is the reason for which it is being done, and the circumstances are the

---

[17] Aquinas, *Summa Theologiae IIa, Q. 18-20*, 210-267.

conditions surrounding the action that also have the potential to change the moral status of the action. While an act can change from good to bad, these qualities cannot change a bad action to good. In other words, when we act, we are communicating not only something about reality but also something about ourselves, and this is what should correspond to the truth. Those acts that don't correspond to truth or are not in accord with right reason are *malum ex quocumque defectu*, evil comes from a single defect.[18] Without this acknowledgment, we live a life that is incompatible with truth and ultimately incompatible with ourselves, which is often why we find ourselves unhappy or unfulfilled when we do something "bad" and happy when we do something "good." Hence, acts of disintegration are bad and contribute to our own disintegration and demise, while acts of integration are good and contribute to our flourishing and true happiness.

In review, because of how the human person was designed, his intellect and will yearn for the truth in

---

[18] The scholastic axiom cited in Aquinas, *Summa Theologiae IIa, Q. 18-20,* 210-267.

matters that reason acquires through natural knowledge. This knowledge, however, is not enough, and he needs the divine light of faith and gift of grace to come to know truth and himself: "Consequently the decisive answer to every one of man's questions, his religious and moral questions in particular, is given by Jesus Christ, or rather is Jesus Christ himself...."[19]

The issues of moral action and morality concern all humanity, regardless of religious status, and this in part is why the Catholic Church remains in the service and protection of all humanity. As the only moral tradition that integrates the whole human person and respects their freedom, she also safeguards the path of the moral life and encourages actions that speak truth well and that always dignify, presenting as the "source and summit of the economy of salvation, as the Alpha and the Omega of human history."[20] Actions that reflect the truth well and that dignify are moral actions in accord with right reason, where every element (object, intention, and circumstance)

---

[19] *Veritatis splendor*, §10.
[20] *Veritatis splendor*, §18.

is intrinsically good, and they are freely chosen. From here, an ethical framework can be developed to live a moral and upright life that is not merely superficial but fully integrated and transformed for the greatness that calls to the depths of our hearts, that is love: "The moral life presents itself as the response due to the many gratuitous initiatives taken by God out of love for man. It is a response of love…" to be primarily lived out by the transcending of oneself through actions beyond that of living for or serving oneself.[21]

In matters related to suffering, where questions of seeking the truth often confront the human person in his unrest and uncertainty, it is only "Christ [that] sheds light on man's condition and his integral vocation."[22] Not only can one guide one's actions, but even in the face of suffering, one can also transform them in ways that could never have been accomplished, providing the afflicted purpose and hope. These delicate and often sensitive matters are expounded upon next.

---

[21] *Veritatis splendor*, §21.
[22] *Veritatis splendor*, §18.

Chapter 4

On Human Suffering and a Call to the Healthcare Professional

Lacrimae Rerum:
"'Oh, Achates,' / he cried, 'is there anywhere,
any place on earth / not filled with our ordeals? ...
even here, the world is
a world of tears / and the burdens of mortality touch the heart ...
My comrades, hardly strangers to pain
before now, / we all have weathered worse.'"

--Virgil's 'The Aeneid'

As I unite the above tearful words as a cry on behalf of all who have suffered or are suffering, I can't help but pause and reflect on the mystery of my own experiences of human suffering, personally and especially through others, on how the "*lacrimae rerum*" affects the human person. In addition to my own painful sufferings and as a longtime medical professional, I have routinely experienced and witnessed the reality of suffering first-hand, and it always continues to move me and fosters continual reflection on such a mysterious reality. Presented to us at the foot of the healthcare bedside are those suffering from illness, pain, isolation, trauma, mental health, but all forms of suffering in life experiences, from individual to collective as a society. Nothing is hidden from view, and humanity often tends to look bleak, unjust, and unfair if such is not kept in perspective.

Nonetheless, it is important to expound upon suffering to see how it affects the human person in their freedom, choices, and outlook. To begin, some general notions on suffering are presented, followed by an overview of how it affects the human person, including the individual aspects that can worsen when the communal aspect is diminished by those who are called to care for others, as well as those who are connected to the circumstances within the life of those suffering.

While universally experienced, no single description can encapsulate what human suffering is or how it is defined. It is quite evident that no one is immune to suffering, and the inescapable experience often leads many to feelings of hopelessness, bitterness, and despair – a seeming suffocation of their very being. It can be different as the individual experiences it regardless of support or status. We even see this within the biological circle of life, albeit experienced on an existential level of awareness known not to vegetative or animal life. Our lives, from the very beginning, slowly begin to deteriorate. It is a:

> temporary staying of death. Every one of our cells is preserved at the cost of an ongoing struggle with forces that tend to destroy it. From our youth, our tissues include large areas subject to deterioration and general wear and tear. From our birth, human cells contain the seeds of their own destruction ... Sickness marks the whole of our fleshly life ...[,][1]

and, therefore, so does suffering. Even in good health, our defense mechanisms can potentially weaken,

---

[1] Marcel Sendrail, *Historie Culturelle de la Maladie*, (Toulouse, 1980), 2.

both physically and mentally. Dismissing a reality that is deeply part of the human condition as if it does not matter would be nonsensical and detrimental.

Human suffering is, indeed, a mystery. It can be acute or chronic. It can come from physical afflictions of the body and/or psychological and spiritual afflictions of the mind, heart, and soul. Psychologically, the effects of experiencing suffering never really escape the memory and often manifest themselves somatically by presenting as physical symptoms within the body.[2] Suffering can impose both physical isolation and a type of mental isolation whereby anxiety, discouragement, anguish, and even despair in confronting the situation develop.

---

[2] Danny Brom, Yaffa Stokar, Cathy Lawi, et al, "Somatic Experiencing for Posttraumatic Stress Disorder: A Randomized Controlled Outcome Study," in *Journal of Traumatic Stress 30(3)*, (June 2017): 310-312 at https://www.ncbi.nlm.nih.gov/pmc/articles/PMC551843; Breanne Kearney and Ruth Lanius, "The Brain-Body Disconnect: A Somatic Sensory Basis for Trauma-Related Disorders," in *Frontiers in Neuroscience Vol. 16* (2022) at https://www.ncbi.nlm.nih.gov/pmc/articles/PMC97201-53.

In general, suffering results from illness, choices, or traumatic circumstances, becomes a threat to human agency or values, is associated with negative feelings, and affects relationships as well as outlook on life. Because suffering feels like an attack on a person's very being, one is led to grapple with inescapable, metaphysical questions about themselves: *Why and why now? What does this mean for the future? Will this end?*

While the events that correspond with physical and mental suffering affect us, regardless of religiosity or spirituality, all are forced to assume a struggle that is higher than ourselves. Hence, Dostoyevsky writes: "A healthy man is always an earthly, material man … But as soon as he falls ill, and the normal, earthly order of his organism is disturbed, then the possibility of another world makes itself known to him at once; and as the illness worsens, his relations with this world become ever closer."[3]

In turn, the experience of suffering causes us to seek care in the other for prevention, counsel, cure,

---

[3] Dostoyevsky, *Crime and Punishment*, (Paris: Gallimard, 1950), 342.

and care through the healing medical profession. In fact, there are multiple fields within science and technology spurred by the effects of illness that are dedicated to assisting others in coping with the certain cruelties that come from extremely fragile and vulnerable states. Modern medicine, modern technology, and expanding scientific knowledge can provide cures and prevention but have never quite been able to provide or acknowledge answers the human person inevitably seeks amid this existential crisis of *meaning*.

This battle, the search for meaning, is acquired by the person experiencing suffering, which stems from human freedom to define the meaning, and here is where the struggle lies. While finding meaning is very personal to one's identity, as a social and communal being the search also draws insights that can be positive or negative through others. When it is not found or negative, the experience is diminished by others, the new identity within one's suffering is subverted, and suffering can quickly turn to the feeling of victimization under the influence and lack of compassion by others. This communal or social aspect of suffering can greatly affect the individual and their story.

To my beloved medical colleagues, who have dedicated your life to the caring and cure of others, often at personal expense:

While not at all fundamentally bad, our healing profession, science, and technology are also experiencing an existential crisis. Too often, the naturalist or physicalist perspectives among us wind up putting bandages on problems through the objectification of illness (mental and physical). This lens sees illness and suffering as uniquely physiological rather than as part of the whole person. As a result of this quantitative and myopic view, only the afflicted organ or body of our patients is treated. When there is suffering, more than the body or physical processes are involved. The entire *person, who they are*, and their very *being* are encompassed and matter. We must see that *being* is beyond the physical; it is metaphysical. The spiritual portion of the human person being confronted and affected is either ignored or not seen as valued. This, in turn, causes even more suffering and isolation in our patients. It is a type of depersonalized outlook that has significant consequences for the care and cure of the underserved and underappreciated aspect of suffering and its effects on the whole human person.

When patients have become divested of their illness and their suffering, with biology and medicine seen as salvation, their means of coping and searching for meaning and purpose is limited by their being treated as merely biological and physiological, or, when considered as a state of well-being, strictly material. As a result, the highest value of the patient then becomes avoiding pain and suffering at all costs; fear and anxiety can develop over the absolute end with biological death, anything that reduces enjoyment becomes considered taboo, any type of suffering is refused, and goals of care then revolve around complete pain relief (which is near impossible). In fact, many of the requests for physician assistance in terminating their own lives include all those reasons. It is no wonder why their request for their decision is associated with the unintended result of depersonalized and devalued care within the healing medical profession, as well as a general misunderstanding of suffering.[4] Needless to say, as healers and as a society we are failing them and contributing to their demise and our own.

It is no wonder mental health incidence rates, including deaths, are consistently increasing.[5] A recent edition of TIME magazine in August of 2023 published the stark reality of mental health getting worse,

---

[4] The top end-of-life concerns are in order: less able to engage in activities making life enjoyable (247), losing autonomy (240), loss of dignity (172), burdensome care (129), loosing control of bodily functions (124), inadequate pain control (87), and financial implications (17) in the "Oregon Death with Dignity Act 2022 Data Summary," (Oregon: Public Health Division, Center for Health Statistics, 8 March 2023), 14, at https://www.oregon.gov/oha/PH/PROVIDERPARTNERRESOURCES/EVALUATIONRESEARCH/DEATHWITHDIGNITYACT/Documents/year25.pdf.

[5] It is important to note, that many physical illnesses have associated mental health challenges. There is a strong correlation between the two; Yang Wu, Lu Wang, Mengiun Tae, et al, "Changing Trends in the Global Burden of Mental Disorders from 1990 to 2019 and Predicted Levels in 25 Years" in *Epidemiology Psychiatry Science*, 32:e63, (7 November 2023), at https://www.ncbi.nlm.nih.gov/pmc/articles/PMC10689059/.

with some experts believing that the issues go much deeper than leaning on therapies and medications. Not all symptoms are related to chemical imbalances, but poor life choices, unhealthy relationships, problematic habits, and lack of problem-solving related to stress: one in eight U.S. adults are on an antidepressant, one in five received some mental-health care, with a 40% jump in mental health services, suicide rates have risen by 20%, and 1/3 of adults report symptoms of depression or anxiety.[6]

Sickness and suffering cannot be regarded as a purely physiological autonomous reality that results in a technical treatment of the body. This does little to support our patients and leaves them at the behest and control of those who care for them. This passive approach to the treatment of suffering encourages illusory attitudes in patients that: "many might escape death ... escape the limits of his present condition, and that he might attain a form of life free of imperfections, where he can grow, free of limitations,"

---

[6] Jamie Ducharme, "America has Reached Peak Therapy. Why is our Mental Health Getting Worse?" in *TIME* Magazine, (28 August 2023), at https://time.com/6308096/therapy-mental-health-worse-us/.

whereby the only solution and hope for relief from their troubles and unendurable suffering is simply medical solutions or ending it all.[7] This is not care or cure.

It is quite evident that years of our seeing and treating the human person as solely a biological entity has done little to address suffering individuals in their illnesses and/or traumatic circumstances. The effects of disregarding the spiritual dimension of the human person have been overwhelmingly negative, including contributing to worsening suffering, as the previously cited evidence strongly suggests. The human person can never be treated in a segmented fashion or considered like every other form of life. Human life simply is not. The human body is a body that:

> cannot be disassociated without losing its very nature. In its present conditions of existence, the body is inseparable not only from a complex psychological element that in itself elevates man well above animals; it is also

---

[7] Jean-Claude Larchet, *The Theology of Illness*, trans by John & Michael Breck, (Crestwood, NY: St. Vladimir's Seminary Press, 2002), 11.

inseparable from a spiritual dimension that is more basic than its biological aspect. The body does not only express the person; to a certain extent it *is* the person.[8]

The failure to see this reality, or see value in it, devalues a person's meaning and/or search for meaning, sets that person up for failure, and leaves him or her unable to withstand future trials and the basic ability to cope with life and its challenges. At these crossroads, it is important to understand how suffering relates to freedom, choice, and moral action, which culminate under the umbrella of truth.

---

[8] Larchet, *The Theology of Illness*, 14.

Chapter 5

How to Suffer Well – How Suffering & Truth Relate to Freedom, Choice, and Moral Action & an Encouragement to those Suffering

While the phrase 'how to suffer well' might seem like an oxymoron, our rational faculties can be quite powerful in providing and even creating meaning in suffering. In this way, a form of redemption to our sufferings is brought, rather than our being tempted to undergo actions that devalue the sacredness of human life and dignity.[1] While this characterization

---

[1] Ontological human dignity is defined as "the indispensable nature" of the human person, which is connected to being created in the image and likeness of God and elevated by Christ. As a result, this has significant implications for society, politics, economics, law, technology, medical care, etc. It is also affirmed in the Universal Declaration of Human Rights, issued by the United Nations General Assembly on 10 December 1948, cf Pope Francis, Declaration On Human Dignity *Dignitas Infinita*, (2 April 2024).

might seem discordant, suffering "well" is not just related to the ability to cope and/or find meaning. Since our choices also correspond to our happiness and supernatural end, the choices we make for ourselves should inevitably correspond to actions that are in accord with the right moral reason and affirm our inherent value as human beings:

> They express the rational order of good and evil impressed into creation. Thus, almsgiving is good because it perfects the almsgiver [and feelings of goodness, happiness, joy, etc, result]. In providing the needs of his neighbor, the individual grows in charity and promotes both his own well-being and the well-being of his neighbor and their human community. ... In contrast, there are acts whose objects are not in conformity with right reason and the moral order. These acts are intrinsically evil because their moral objects ... radically contradict the good of the person ... [and] do not promote the perfection of the individual human being ... For instance, murder is evil because it is an act of injustice. The murderer

deprives another individual of the life that is rightfully his [and the result is experienced in continued aggression and displacement of heart] ... These moral absolutes, usually articulated in the form of commandments, are ordered towards the realization of human excellence and beatitude. They are guides that help us to live fulfilling and holy lives.[2]

Without personally acknowledging suffering well and their connections, we inevitably find ourselves enveloped in emotional and psychological slavery to our own thoughts and situations. On the surface, understandably finding little to no joy in our current newly acquired state and clinging to the notion of 'no way out,' we are then led to a downward spiral of resentment, anxiety, paralyzing despair, powerlessness, worsening pain, and continued depression.[3] In

---

[2] Austriaco, *Biomedicine & Beatitude*, 31-32.
[3] See footnote 55; Paul Wong & Timothy Yu, "Existential Suffering in Palliative Care: An Existential Positive Psychology Perspective," in *Medicina* 57(9), (September 2021), 924 at https://www.ncbi.nlm.nih.gov/pmc/articles/PMC8471755/.

moments of immense vulnerability, we forget our impressive ability to exercise choice in the challenging moments and what to do with that choice. This is worse if we are alone and/or have no support. We must learn to withstand the challenges of suffering skillfully, or it will undermine our ability to enjoy life, and we will cease to be able to help others undergoing similar trials.

Simultaneously, we may also try to find misconceived healing by choosing actions that do not have our ultimate good in mind. We end up pursuing ends in order to fill our buckets with waters of happiness, but have holes because what we are pursuing is not lasting happiness. Evidence of this on a small scale is seen in our daily life of "things and desires." The new car, handbag, Facebook 'likes,' largest house, and latest gadget may increase our happiness for a short while, but then we fall back to our own baseline level of happiness. It does not matter what or how much you have, what you choose to invest your time in, or any other fill-in-the-blank to satisfy the treadmill of hedonic living. After all, "life on earth is not an 'ultimate' but a 'penultimate' reality; even so, it remains a sacred reality entrusted to us, to be preserved with a sense of responsibility and brought to perfection in love and in the gift of ourselves to God and to our brothers and sisters," and creation.[4] If we are not living in ways we should or are not choosing for ourselves ways of lasting value and purpose, we will forever be in a perpetual cycle of self-loathing and misery when confronted with real suffering.

On a larger scale and in society, we see this in two ways. The first is in attempts to control our situation rather than accept it, thereby inflicting pain and suffering on others through our own actions motivated by love of self:

> A certain idea of this problem comes to us from the distinction between physical suffering and moral suffering. This distinction is based upon the double dimension of the human being and indicates the bodily and spiritual element as the immediate or direct subject of suffering. Insofar as the words "suffering" and "pain", can, up to a certain degree, be

---

[4] John Paul II, The Gospel of Life *Evangelium vitae* (25 March 1995), §2 (Boston: Saint Paul Books & Media, 1995), 14.

used as synonyms, physical suffering is present when "the body is hurting" in some way, whereas moral suffering is "pain of the soul". In fact, it is a question of pain of a spiritual nature, and not only of the "psychological" dimension of pain which accompanies both moral and physical suffering. The vastness and the many forms of moral suffering are certainly no less in number than the forms of physical suffering. But at the same time, moral suffering seems as it were less identified and less reachable by therapy. [5]

---

[5] John Paul II, On the Meaning of Human Suffering *Salvifici Doloris* (11 February 1984), §5; Orthodox psychotherapy also views illness, and the associated unrest present in the mind and heart that results thereof, in the form of self-love, which maintains that "when someone's soul is dominated by passion, which are mainly the unnatural impulses of the powers of the soul, and when he is unable to see God as Light, he is spiritually ill," Metropolitan of Nafpaktos Hierotheos, *The Science of Spiritual Medicine: Orthodox Psychotherapy in Action*, trans. by Sister Pelagia Selfe, (Greece: Birth of Theotokos Monastery, 2010), 87.

Ch. 5: How to Suffer Well

The second way is by choosing perceived "goods" that are counter to natural law and violate the sanctity of human life and dignity; we fail to see value in moments of suffering being inflicted on us, befallen to us, or outside and as a result of our own actions.[6] In

---

[6] Perceived 'goods' chosen for ourselves or we inflict on others in moments of weakness and/or vulnerability are those that are counter to natural and violate the sanctity of human life and dignity are as follows: 'Whatever is opposed to life itself, such as any type of murder, genocide, abortion, euthanasia, or wilful self-destruction, whatever violates the integrity of the human person, such as mutilation, torments inflicted on body or mind, attempts to coerce the will itself; whatever insults human dignity, such as subhuman living conditions, arbitrary imprisonment, deportation, slavery, prostitution, the selling of women and children; as well as disgraceful working conditions, where people are treated as mere instruments of gain rather than as free and responsible persons; all these things and others like them are infamies indeed. They poison human society, and they do more harm to those who practise them than to those who suffer from the injury.' Unfortunately, this disturbing state of affairs, far from decreasing, is expanding: with the new prospects opened up by scientific and technological progress there arise new forms of attacks on the dignity of the human being,' *Evangelium vitae*, §4.

other words, by failing to preserve our dignity and life through action, we exclude ourselves from experiencing the resiliency that was meant for us to create ourselves anew through trials and opportunities presented to us. We see perceived 'goods' in the world through our kaleidoscope glasses, but these leave us and those around us ultimately more wounded and distant from what we thought might make us happier or more relieved at the time.

In modern psychology, researchers have studied concepts such as resiliency, post-traumatic growth, and existential positive psychology, which claim to employ a new "science of suffering" that integrates the bright and darker sides of life, including the unknown fear of death.[7] This integrated, bidirectional approach to suffering is "essential for creating a more complete picture of human flourishing, just as the science of pain and disease control is essential for physical health and medical science."[8] In these life-changing moments, creating new pathways for purpose,

---

[7] Tedeschi & Calhoun, *Trauma & Transformation*, 1995; Wong, er al., "Shifting the Paradigm," 13–27.

[8] Arslan and Wong, "Measuring Personal and Social Responsibility," 1-11.

and resiliency, or post-traumatic growth, is a part of this process. One might even say that on a fundamental level, we need to experience various types of suffering in order to change and grow or realize that our actions or ways of living are not as virtuous as they should be.

Resiliency, and awareness of the importance of our actions being aligned with the objective moral good, are indeed key within suffering and moral action, as they require choosing self-transcendence and ways of virtue, no matter the cause. In other words, as rational and free creatures, we can still actively choose to find purpose and value, which will help us persevere despite our sufferings and feelings of enslavement.

Viktor Frankl, a psychiatrist and Holocaust survivor, wrote extensively while in concentration camps about this process. He observed that fellow inmates were more likely to survive horrific conditions if they held on to a strong sense of meaning. For instance, exposing one's vulnerability, tragedy, and experiences can raise self-confidence and strength, deepen relationships and appreciation of life, cause growth in beliefs, and provide new opportunities.[9] In some senses, one might say that through trials and tribulations, suffering can create a new and better creation in the person: "Through pain, a new being is born. Pain creates the right conditions for another world, previously invisible to us, to open up."[10]

In addition to finding personal purpose and value through the witness of persevering within an afflicted state, one can provide accompaniment to those going through similar experiences. This witnessing truly gives meaning to the *com* in *compassion*.[11] There are countless personal and collective examples of the power of witnessing to others through perseverance

---

[9] A car crash survivor reported after the incident that it caused her to take charge of her life, and as a result, she had greater will power, and others often feel empowered to help others and create change; De Sales Turner and Helen Cox, "Facilitating Post Traumatic Growth" in *Health Quality of Life Outcomes* Vol. 2, 34 (2004) at https://hqlo.biomedcentral.com/articles/10.1186/1477-7525-2-34#citeas.

[10] Hierotheos, *The Science of Spiritual Medicine*, 194.

[11] The Latin meaning of compassion is "compassio," which means to "suffer with" from "Online Etymology Dictionary at https://www.etymonline.com/word/compassion.

in adversity. We all experience it on varying levels when we see those struggling to continue to carry on and keep up with daily life. We become inspired to do the same through observing the other transforming themselves anew.[12] Inspiration evokes within us the transcendent, which rises above the self and the passions, and involves a moment of clarity and awareness leading to a newer vision of ourselves, one we once thought might never be possible. We are then able to move to act in light of that inspiration. This, however, is only seen through the other, through a form of participation in common society, as we do not live alone but with others: "In this anthropology, the concept 'participation' indicates that man, when acting with others, keeps the personalistic value of his own action and at the same time affects the realization and results of the common action."[13]

---

[12] Todd Thrash, Laura Maruskin, Scott Cassidy, et. al, "Mediating Between the Muse and the Masses: Inspiration and the Actualization of Creative Ideas" in *Journal of Personality and Social Psychology, 98(3)*, 469–487 at https://doi.org/10.1037/a0017907.

[13] Acosta and Reimers, *Karol Wojtyla*, 227.

To all those who are suffering:

While our natural capacity for perseverance can certainly provide resiliency and inspiration, it does not allow us to discover the full meaning of suffering. This is why we must look to Revelation of Divine Love, which expresses the transcendent destination for which we are made, which is love: "Love is also the richest source of the meaning of suffering, which always remains a mystery … Christ causes us to enter into the mystery and to discover the 'why' of suffering, as far as we are capable of grasping the sublimity of divine love, which makes itself present in God's gift to man in the Cross of Jesus Christ."[14]

---

[14] *Salvifici doloris,* §13.

Chapter 6

Redemptive Suffering, Inspiration, and Joyful Triumph

"I sometimes wish I were suffering in a good cause, or risking my life for the good of others, instead of just being a gravely endangered patient."

– Atheist Christopher Hitchens, reflecting over his long battle with cancer. [1]

We may never understand why an innocent child suffers from leukemia or a child grows up in an abusive environment while a person who commits various evils thrives. While this is not meant to diminish the personalization of individualized suffering, the stark reality is that everyone suffers, and it is the very question of desiring to know the reasons and meaning that contribute to our suffering. We live in a world

---

[1] Christopher Hitchens, "Topic of Cancer," *Vanity Fair*, Sept. 2010, https://www.vanityfair.com/culture/2010/09/hitchens-201009.

where fortunes and misfortunes seem extremely unfair, muddled, and fraught with the challenge of finding a deeper meaning. As Christopher Hitchens, an atheist, honestly reflects above upon this universal existential struggle. Yet, it is suffering that somehow has the ability to unlock the very meaning of life and ourselves:

> Suffering as it were contains a special call to the virtue which man must exercise on his own part. And this is the virtue of perseverance in bearing whatever disturbs and causes harm. In doing this, the individual unleashes hope, which maintains in him the conviction that suffering will not get the better of him, that it will not deprive him of his dignity as a human being, a dignity linked to awareness of the meaning life.[2]

This reality of meaning, however, is far from complete. What is missing in our world and individual lives is the beginning and the end of our story, which

---

[2] *Salvifici doloris,* §23.

can remind us of our profound dignity beyond the pain from suffering experienced. This meaning becomes fulfilled if we but open our pained and weary hearts to the depths of the inexplicable love story for you and me seen at the *crossroads* of redemption, lifted by an earthly inspiration, and ultimately ending in triumphant joy.

Contrary to how it may feel or what people think, while circumstances often seem heartless, calculated, and cold, they are certainly not caused by an evil, clockwork Creator who winds up our lives and lets the cards land where they may, abandoning us to our own situations. Our free will is respected way too much to be controlled like a puppet. We are foolish to forget that even we can be responsible for inflicting suffering on ourselves and others through our actions, obstinacy, or failures. Affirming a puppet master mentality or denying our role in our own demise would imply a lack of free will, and this simply isn't the case. Our responsibility aside, even in our failings and stupidities, we are considered good, and resulting unpleasantries or sufferings are opportunities for growth.

Our beginning is explained in the Christian anthropological study of our original existence and helps us understand this meaning. Despite its current failings and misgivings, humanity was originally made good and designed to be happy, as is the human person.[3] In fact, there was perfect happiness.[4] After separation from the One who brought us into existence, it was suffering that was experienced: "Neither illness nor deformity existed in the beginning with our [original] nature."[5] While there was the capacity to suffer, the experience of suffering was lacking, as we were not separated from the goodness from and for which we were created. We, however, suffer because of a certain lack, limit, or distorted good of the intellect, as suffering is "something evil to the extent that it arises as a consequence of the sin of Adam."[6]

---

[3] Genesis 1:26-31; *Salvifici doloris,* §10.

[4] Referring to Thomas Aquinas and the Beatific Vision that we once had, cf footnote 8.

[5] This separation is also referred to as "the Fall;" Larchet, *The Theology of Illness,* 21; St. Gregory of Nyssa in *Homilies on the Statues* XI, 2 and *On Virginity* XII, 2 in Larchet, *The Theology of Illness*, 19.

[6] Larchet, *The Theology of Illness,* 56; *Salvifici doloris,* §7; *CCC,* 376.

The end of our story, which refers to our Final End, purpose, and reason for being made, is Love.[7] It is only with the gift of faith, through the same grace that was once present, that these actions can have true merit and redemption, thus providing authentic healing.[8] Even Victor Frankl and Nietzsche weren't too far from this same understanding by saying that "He who has a *why* to live for can bear with almost any *how*."[9] It is faith and the gift of grace that give us this *why*. Events that cause anger and despair, as well as the suffering and pain that come from them, can now result in goodness that has the meaning of God's work and providence.[10] Without this, there is no purpose, direction, or meaning.

Like the men who experienced great suffering in the Auschwitz concentration camps, a higher, redemptive meaning comes with the choice to accept

---

[7] *Salvifici doloris,* §13.

[8] The grace referred to here is the grace of Baptism, cf *CCC*, 1214-1228.

[9] Frankl's quotation from Nietzsche in "Oxford Essential Quotations," 5 ed., (Oxford University Press, 2017), at https://www.oxfordreference.com/display/10.1093/acref/9780191843730.001.0001/q-oro-ed5-00007886.

[10] *CCC*, 302.

one's suffering and refuse to give up hope instead of escaping into a condition of passivity, numbness, or annihilation. Clinging to higher levels of spiritual integrity under intense circumstances can help one realize higher levels of spiritual freedom and purpose in the midst of darkness and deprivation. In fact, in one passage, Frankl told of those who, though they were starving, chose to give their last bits of food to help others, and thus realize the ultimate sacrifice of choosing to take up one's cross for the sake of another. Ultimately, this added significant meaning to their otherwise hopeless situation and offered them an opportunity to grow beyond themselves spiritually. Following the moving passage of those giving what little they had to others, Victor Frankl wrote the following long, yet powerful excerpt.

> Everything can be taken from a man but one thing: the last of the human freedoms – to choose one's attitude in any given set of circumstances, to choose one's own way. ...in the final analysis it becomes clear that the sort of person the prisoner became was the result of an inner decision, and not the result of

camp influences alone. Fundamentally, therefore, any man can, even under such circumstances, decide what shall become of him – mentally and spiritually ... the way they bore their suffering was a genuine inner achievement. It is this spiritual freedom—which cannot be taken away—that makes life meaningful and purposeful.

An active life serves the purpose of giving man the opportunity to realize values in creative work, while a passive life of enjoyment affords him the opportunity to obtain fulfillment in experiencing beauty, art, nature. But there is also purpose in that life which is almost barren of both creation and enjoyment and which admits of but one possibility of high moral behavior: namely in man's attitude to this existence, an existence restricted by eternal forces. ...If there is meaning in life at all, then there must be a meaning in suffering. Suffering is an ineradicable part of life, even as fate and death. Without suffering and death human life cannot be complete.

> The way in which a man accepts his fate and all the suffering it entails, the way in which he takes up his cross, gives him ample opportunity—even under the most difficult circumstances—to add a deeper meaning to his life.[11]

Each of us has this same power that Victor expounds upon if we only look beyond ourselves and cling to the spiritual part that calls upon us for greatness through redemption. However, this ability to find meaning becomes harder when we lack the gift and support of grace and faith.

From a Catholic Christian perspective, Christ is everything, including that power made present in his sacraments of the Church and made present in a limited way through others' compassion and mercy. This faith in Jesus Christ is far from merely "spiritual," as it is only made possible through the physical relationship of God becoming man, who is also our Physician and Healer. Our suffering becomes an opportunity to

---

[11] Victor Frankl, *Man's Search for Meaning*, (New York, NY: Simon & Schuster, 1919), 86-88.

draw closer to Christ, suffer with him, find redemptive meaning in our suffering, and even allow that suffering to be a vehicle for further redemption in this world.

While still remaining divine and becoming human, like ourselves, in taking on that humanity and its associated sufferings, his suffering and sacrifice transformed, yielding our own redemption and healing. The most significant form of physical suffering and torment was what Christ experienced on the cross and the internal suffering experienced by his mother the moment she said "yes."

Moments of evil and suffering can be made anew and given hope through Christ, as he "took suffering upon himself and sanctified it. He changed it from an evil to a good."[12] Here, we find a new light shed on the world and humanity in their suffering state. We see this perfectly in the mission and teachings of Jesus Christ during his life and in the example he lived towards his human end: "…his actions concerned primarily those who were suffering and seeking help. He

---

[12] Hubert Van Zeller, *The Mystery of Suffering*, (Notre Dame, IN: Christian Classics, 2015), 9.

healed the sick, consoled the afflicted, fed the hungry … He was sensitive to every human suffering, whether of the body or of the soul."[13] In every encounter, he entered into the lives of others to accompany, and not only experience whatever they were going through, but also experience it himself within his physical body: homelessness (Lk 9:58), isolation (Jn 7:11), hostility (Jn 7:11), rejection (Jn 6:67), mental distress (Mt 26:36-46), abandonment (Mt 27:46), fatigue (Mk 4:37-40), and pain (Lk 22:63-65).

He lived through every form of suffering we can imagine and more, which for us should inspire a deeper communion and solidarity with humankind. Like a father and mother who stays up all night in a hospital to comfort their sick child, or in order to provide strength merely through their presence, climbs into an ice bath with their little one to cool their small body, so, too, did Christ. In his humanity, he embodied the perfect character within the human dimension of how he suffers with us through the stages of his Passion: including suffering innocently (see the medical claims of these sufferings in the footnotes

---

[13] *Salvifici doloris*, §16.

below for further clarity), "the arrest, the humiliation, the blows, the spitting, the contempt for the prisoner, the unjust sentence, ... the scourging, the crowning with thorns, ... the mocking, the carrying of the Cross, the crucifixion and the agony."[14] All of these

---

[14] *Salvifici doloris,* §17; Pierre Barbet, in *A Doctor at Calvary: The Passion of the Our Lord Jesus Christ Described by a Surgeon,* (New York: Image Books, 1963), 69, 91, provides medical claims for the sweating of blood, known as hematidrosis, which is associated with great intensity and mental anguish of the type of suffering he underwent; the torture device of scouring that was used was composed of two balls made from the small bone of a sheep, which led to the following injuries of blunt chest trauma whose effects are common knowledge within the medical field: pneumothorax, pleural effusion, chest pain, splinting, flail chest, pulmonary contusion, shock, blunt cardiac trauma, heart damage, pericardial injuries, hyperkalemia, and dehydration. Dr. Thomas McGovern, M.D. in *What Christ Suffered* reminds us that the robe worn when the guards stripped him after the scourging was likely dried from those wounds and the masses of clotted blood, skin, and muscle were reopened; the weight of the part of the cross that was laid over him alone was 75-125 lbs and carried around the length of a high school track after tremendous pains from previous wounds; limited sleep of being up for the past 32 hours, no food, which alone can cause intense nausea, vomiting, and weakness; the pounding of nails

the human person has encountered in some form, albeit, limited. Jesus' suffering and death show us that not only does he take on all the sufferings of humanity in body and soul, but also that his suffering provides Redemption from our original failure in the beginning so that we might be truly healed: "Christ has accomplished the world's Redemption through his own suffering."[15]

If Christ provides redemptive suffering, then the one who bore him, raised him, and watched him suffered as well. His Mother, our Blessed Mother Mary, provides a model and inspiration for responding to the sufferings that befall us. One might say that Christ, the Physician, gives us the perfect prescript-

---

into flesh would have to be supported by bone; and death by the culminating result of everything experienced and ending in a terminal arrhythmia: hemorrhagic and hypovolemic shock, respiratory muscle fatigue, trauma-coagulopathy, and metabolic acidosis (Huntington, Indiana: Our Sunday Visitor, 2020), 115, 127, 134, 166, 174, and 201.

[15] What is meant by "taking on" is that our many sufferings, by uniting them to his sufferings on the Cross, can be used for good and for the salvation of oneself and for others. *Salvifici doloris,* §24.

ion and remedy for our ills, as he tells Peter to put away his sword: "Shall I not drink the chalice which the Father has given me?" (Jn 18:11), and his Mother provides the example of long-term suffering, which was inflicted on her the moment she said "yes" to the news of her being with child. Her whole life bears this mark that culminated in an intense way during her Son's Passion: "In her, the many and intense sufferings were amassed in such an interconnected way that they were not only a proof of her unshakable faith but also a contribution to the redemption of all."[16]

In complete vulnerability, I would like to offer two of many virtuous qualities within Mary that have been an inspiration to me as one who suffers from painful endometriosis, infertility, habits of negative views of self from past eating disorders, and often overwhelmed feelings of hopelessness within my own profession in the care of another: compassion and humble fidelity. Both are strongly connected. Compassion, or co-suffering, involves the will to suffer with the other, and humble fidelity requires long-

---

[16] *Salvifici doloris,* §25.

term faithfulness with an open heart. We know that throughout Mary's life, she continuously suffered. Her sufferings, however, were heightened and intensified when they were made manifest through words of the flesh when it was originally predicted by Simeon and experienced on Calvary.

To explain these two qualities, I would like to use the Seven Sorrows of Mary, which are traditionally held by St. Bridget of Sweden.[17] The first and fourth through seventh sword thrusts embody her perfect compassion, despite her immense sorrow "[as] she walks it with the entire human sorrow of a human mother who must be present at her son's end."[18] Gazing at the tiny and innocent body of her infant, only to eventually be torn, wounded, and beaten, she knew in her heart what was to befall him in his adulthood.

---

[17] St. Bridget, "Devotion to Our Lady of Sorrows," at https://carmelitesistersocd.com/devotion-to-our-lady-of-sorrows/: Prophecy of Simeon, Flight into Egypt, Loss of the Child Jesus for Three Days, Meeting of Jesus on Calvary, Crucifixion, Jesus Taken Down from the Cross, and Jesus Laid in the Tomb.

[18] Adrienne von Speyr, *Handmaid of the Lord*, (San Fransisco, CA: Ignatius Press, 1985), 133; "Seven Sorrows of Mary," according to St. Bridget of Sweden.

It was then confirmed in full intensity as she accompanied, co-suffered with her Son: "[S]o now in her compassion, the pains of martyrdom are first in her soul and only then in her sympathetic flesh, which echoed to every scourge that fell on her Son's back or pierced his hands and feet ... Every pulse in his tiny wrist would sound like the echo of an oncoming hammer."[19]

Secondly, humble fidelity was witnessed through the second and third, as well as the first, piercings. From infancy to her Son's death, she remained ever-faithful in what was being asked for the sake of our sufferings and misgivings. In the second and third, we see the anxiety of fleeing during the flight into Egypt and the anguish of a lost child until he was found in the temple: "[T]his second thrust used the instrumentality of wicked men" and a foretaste of the future loss that was to become of her Son at a later time that would be revealed.[20] She could have remained in Bethlehem and, likewise, abandoned her role as a mother of someone she knew she would lose

---

[19] Fulton Sheen, *The World's First Love*, (San Francisco, CA: Ignatius Press, 1996), 243-244.

[20] Sheen, *The World's First Love*, 245.

again, but in a more permanent way. With patience and endurance, however, she bore her cross with humble fidelity. She welcomed the plan laid before her, knowing what greater mission was at stake for the world: "She has tasted, [loss], abandonment and loneliness. And she knows that he is God and, as God, survives all destruction and death. [While she certainly believed it, s]he cannot imagine the Resurrection, nor does she picture the future to herself. She has only faith, which overcomes every death."[21]

Thus, it can be said with confidence what can become of us in our sufferings, quite literally and figurately: our many labors are born in patience and endurance through our sufferings. When they are conjoined with her Son's Passion and offered to others in total humble fidelity, we, too, can yield similar fruit. This fruit, planted in us by the seed of grace and grown with the water of faith, can provide meaning and nourishment for other struggling wayfarers.

Like her belief in what was humanly impossible at the Annunciation, we, too, submit our similar *fiat* during times when we do not fully comprehend our

---

[21] Speyr, *Handmaid*, 154.

own sufferings, including those we witness. We look to her Son as we try to endure, and we look to her for her humble attitude and courage through our response that is simple, yet profound. This response, in many senses, becomes incarnational in our free assent within that continued choice of 'yes' in accepting our own crosses and sufferings, which correspond to the similar ascent of Mary's 'yes' and steadfast presence on Calvary.

Finally, there is the joyful triumph that we hope to experience because of and in Christ's Resurrection. On the natural level, we experience this in a limited way in the sense of accomplishment after what we thought was impossible in our struggle but is no longer. When under the umbrella of grace, however, this joy can be elevated and enveloped in shades of hope from the burning weight of the heat amid our trials and tribulations: "A source of joy is found in the overcoming of the sense of the uselessness of suffering, a feeling that is sometimes very strongly rooted in human suffering. … The discovery of the salvific meaning of suffering in union with Christ transforms this depressing feeling."[22] This joy-filled hope can only be found at the end of our rainbow of tears as we await with great anticipation for what has been promised to those who follow Him through the barren desert of life.

There is also joyful triumph found within doing good by our suffering. The primary means of doing good by our suffering is finding purpose in it, such as offering it up as a voluntary sacrifice for others. When we do this and unite them to Calvary, we can contribute to the redemption of others, including providing positive inspiration. As Victor Frankl spoke about the persecuted individuals finding their burden a little lighter after identifying a higher purpose when living for the other, we, too, can find joy in this same way. Yet again, the crucial way in the moments of opportunity is found in a simple, faithful, yet most challenging 'yes.' Only then, in these moments, are we allowed a small taste of the joy in the Resurrection and of what is waiting. What could be better than our suffering being turned into joy?

---

[22] *Salvifici doloris*, §27.

Conclusion
"Talitha koum"[1]

Ultimately, the health of the soul is infinitely more important than the health of the body, and this is why it is important to live lives in truth through our actions and find hope even in suffering. While it is often seen as something to be avoided and rarely feels as if it expands our horizons as we feel the walls closing in, it allows us to do just that, forcing us to take a long look at the mountaintops of our lives, which are connected to the spiritual reality of needing something beyond ourselves that is more meaningful and satisfying. This need forces us to come to grips with our own identity and our own boundaries of "self" in a way that no one else can experience. It must be endured and shared in a limited way with the other in order to overcome. We do not need to live in obsessive fear by running like a madman who seeks to catch immortality by force; we can admit that life has an end, but it is not our soul's end if we respond to

---

[1] "Little girl, I say to you, arise!" See full Scripture verse at the end (Mark 5:21-43).

life's extremely challenging moments through surrendering well with the gift of grace and the Catholic faith. Yet, in these delicate and often humiliating moments, we are allowed the gift to gaze into our own mortality; our transcendent hearts inherently know the glory of the sunrise of new hope as the daylight fades, day in and day out. Here, suffering challenges us to give birth to new meaning, purpose, witness, and perspective. Here, we are called to stretch the ocean view of our souls wide within the drama of turmoil.

While being constantly blessed by the valiant efforts of medicine to treat pain and manage suffering effectively, if regard for the soul is not appreciated, we risk approaching these matters in a way that is unsatisfactory to the human heart and leads to further languishing. We also diminish the capacity for great action of those who have become incapacitated. While they may not be able to serve or live in ways that once seemed fulfilling (or maybe they never could), they are allowing the great privilege of others serving and caring for them. They are also providing an opportunity in their humble assent of mind through faith with the aid of grace to offer up the circumstances that have befallen them for others and their own salvation. Without the ability to act in this way by offering our sufferings up, uniting them to Jesus Christ, we rob ourselves of the full potential to love. This love causes us to sacrifice and transcend ourselves for the sake of the other, in some senses allowing us to be created anew. Therefore, every attempt to escape, diminish completely, or live an invulnerable life in anxiety and fear ultimately betrays and causes weariness, which inevitably distracts us from the graces that lie in wait:

> Remember that bees, during the time in which they make honey, live on a very bitter kind of nourishment, and that in like manner we can never more properly elicit the great acts of meekness and patience, or better compose the honey of excellent virtues, than when we eat the bitter bread of tribulation and live in the midst of anguish. And as that honey which is made from the flowers of thyme, a small but bitter herb, is the best of all, so that virtue which is formed in the bitterness of pain and humiliation is the most

excellent of all. Tribulation and sickness are well calculated to advance us in virtue, on account of the many resignations which they oblige us to make into the hand of Our Lord.[2]

A brilliant bright orange or red leaf, a blossomed tree that begins to fade as the seasons progress; all the beauty seen within nature that climaxes before dying in magnificent color, or painted or composed masterpieces of art within the final chapters of our lives—what beauty or masterpiece will he then bring our lives in our vulnerable moments?

Vulnerability is not weakness, nor does it result in loss of dignity. It is filled with potential and meaning that can create communion and intimate relationships with the other as well as be salvific. While we may be tempted to draw back or resist, if we take that one extra leap of faith and lean into its reverent mystery, the Christian faith in the Catholic moral tradition invites us to discover hope and sustains us in our journey with the necessary food found within the

---

[2] Saint Francis DeSales, *Consoling Thoughts on Sickness and Death*, complied by Pere Huguet, (Charlotte, NC: TAN Books, 2013), 3-4.

sacraments of the Church. This process, while long and grueling at times, is not something to fear or control as much as it is to learn to respond to humbly through our choices aligned with truth, both internally and externally, living with trust. Indeed, moments of anxiety and sadness in our vulnerability can be transformed into sacredness and beauty as we await that final moment when we stand face-to-face with Beauty himself, and suffering is no more. These moments of compiled graces are not filled with a lack of purpose or meaning but with the opportunity to discover appreciation and gratitude that will find us recreating ourselves and becoming a strengthening lamp for others through our daily offerings of these moments. Indeed, this is the universal call to holiness found within suffering and the heroic witnessing that can accompany through graces extended: the willingness through our choices to trust in providential care as we fight the good fight and finish the race of life.

Neither our Lord nor his Blessed Mother shied away from their suffering. In fact, both willingly accepted them with open arms. Publicly, often seen as a failure, both suffered in ways we do, albeit on varying levels and reasons. And yet, we can find comfort and example in each as they continuously made themselves vulnerable, as they offer themselves to us in their own way in the sacraments of the Church (our Lord) and through intercession on our behalf (our Blessed Mother). These ways teach us how to live our sufferings and vulnerability as they do, in a gift that overflows through communion and intimate relationship with the other, which is ultimately with the Father. This gift is not only for us, but also for the redemption of the whole world.

My humble prayer, continued plea, and reminder to myself: "*Alas! Our Savior counted all your sorrows, all your sufferings, and purchased, at the price of His blood, the patience and the love that were necessary for you, in order to worthily refer your pains to His glory and your own salvation.*"[3] Be consoled that there is a higher plan and purpose. As we go through trials in the horizons and mountains of our life, let us listen deeply to the words of Aeneas and weary pilgrim within the lines of Keats' *Ode*. Through little deaths and sufferings each day, there is, indeed, a God who is there to meet us on this challenging pilgrimage that

---

[3] De Sales, *Consoling Thoughts*, 6.

Conclusion: "Talitha koum"

will reveal to us the heights and depths to which love can go and be found. May our lives, through our free actions aligned with truth, attitudes of trust, and expectant hope, become the inspired paintings and compositions that God intends. We must be like Jairus, who asked Jesus to heal his daughter and have faith like the hemorrhaging woman who reached out and touched his robe for healing through his grace. We must let our own vulnerabilities and sufferings draw us ever closer to a relationship and communion with him, who is "our strength and shield" (Psalm 28:7) and *Talitha koum*:

> *And when Jesus had crossed again in the boat to the other side, a great crowd gathered about him; and he was beside the sea. Then came one of the rulers of the synagogue, Ja'irus by name; and seeing him, he fell at his feet, and besought him, saying, "My little daughter is at the point of death. Come and lay your hands on her, so that she may be made well, and live." And he went with him. And a great crowd followed him and thronged about him. And there was a woman who had had a flow of blood for twelve*

years, and who had suffered much under many physicians, and had spent all that she had, and was no better but rather grew worse. She had heard the reports about Jesus, and came up behind him in the crowd and touched his garment. For she said, "If I touch even his garments, I shall be made well." And immediately the hemorrhage ceased; and she felt in her body that she was healed of her disease. And Jesus, perceiving in himself that power had gone forth from him, immediately turned about in the crowd, and said, "Who touched my garments?" And his disciples said to him, "You see the crowd pressing around you, and yet you say, 'Who touched me?'" And he looked around to see who had done it. But the woman, knowing what had been done to her, came in fear and trembling and fell down before him, and told him the whole truth. And he said to her, "Daughter, your faith has made you well; go in peace, and be healed of your disease." Mark 5:21-43)

Bibliography

Acosta, Miguel and Adrian Reimers. *Karol Wojtyla's Personalist Philosophy: Understanding Person & Act*. (Washington, D.C: Catholic University of America Press, 2016).

Aristotle's Metaphysics in Standford Encyclopedia of Philosophy. (8 October 2000), at https://plato.stanford.edu/entries/aristotle-metaphysics/.

Aristotle. *Nicomachean Ethics 113b, Bk III, 5*. Trans W.D. Ross in *The Basic Works of Aristotle*. (New York: Random House, 1941).

Arslan, Gokmen and Paul Wong. "Measuring Personal and Social Responsibility: An Existential Positive Psychology Approach." *Journal of Happiness and Health 2* (2021): 1–11, at *Google Scholar*, https://scholar.google.com/scholar_lookup.

Aquinas, Thomas. *De Veritate* I, at https://catholiclibrary.org/library/view?docId=/MedievalEN/XCT.024.html&chunk.id= 00000561, I.

Aquinas, Thomas. *Summa Theologiae Ia, Q. 83, a.1*. Trans by Fathers of the English Dominican Province. (London: Burns Oates & Washbourne Ltd, 1922).

Austriaco, Nicanor. *Biomedicine & Beatitude: An Introduction to Catholic Bioethics.* (Washington, D.C.: Catholic University of America Press, 2011).

Bandu, Din, Murali Mohan, Noel Nittala, et al. "Theories of Motivation: A Comprehensive Analysis of Human Behavior Drivers." *Acta Psychologica.* Vol. 244. (April 2024), at https://doi.org/10.1016/j.actpsy.2024.104177.

Barbet, Pierre. *A Doctor at Calvary: The Passion of the Our Lord Jesus Christ Described by a Surgeon.* (New York: Image Books, 1963).

Botturi, Francesco. "Liberta e formazione morali," in *Alla Ricercar delle Parole: La Familglia e il Problema Educativo.* Trans. in Google Translate, ed. G. Borgonovo. (Casale Monferrato: Piemme, 2000).

Brom, Danny, Yaffa Stokar, Cathy Lawi, et al. "Somatic Experiencing for Posttraumatic Stress Disorder: A Randomized Controlled Outcome Study." in *Journal of Traumatic Stress 30(3).* (June 2017): 310-312, at https://www.ncbi.nlm.nih.gov/pmc/articles/PMC5518443/.

Catechism of the Catholic Church. 2nded. (Washington, D.C.: United States Catholic Conference, 2000).

Dostoyevsky. *Crime and Punishment.* (Paris: Gallimard, 1950).

Ducharme, Jamie. "America has Reached Peak Therapy. Why is our Mental Health Getting Worse?" in *TIME* Magazine. (28 August 2023), at https://time.com/6308096/therapymental-health-worse-us/.

Frankl, Victor. *Man's Search for Meaning.* (New York, NY: Simon & Schuster, 1919).

Guyer, Paul. "Immanuel Kant: Key Concepts - A Philosophical Introduction," edited by Will Dudley. (Acumen Publishing, 2010).

Hitchens, Christopher. "Topic of Cancer" in *Vanity Fair*. September 2010. https://www.vanityfair.com/culture/2010/09/hitchens-201009.

John Paul II. The Gospel of Life *Evangelium vitae* (25 March 1995), §2 (Boston: Saint Paul Books & Media, 1995).

John Paul II. Encyclical Faith and Reason *Fides et ratio* (14 September 1998).

John Paul II. The Splendor of Truth *Veritatis splendor*. (Boston, MA: Pauline Books & Media. 2003).

Kearney, Breanne and Ruth Lanius. "The Brain-Body Disconnect: A Somatic Sensory Basis for Trauma-Related Disorders" in *Frontiers in Neuroscience Vol. 16* (2022), at https://www.ncbi.nlm.nih.gov/pmc/articles/PMC9720153/.

Larchet, Jean-Claude. *The Theology of Illness*. Trans by John & Michael Breck. (Crestwood, NY: St. Vladimir's Seminary Press, 2002).

Lumintang, Stevri and Benyamin Intan. "Theology and Science: An Analytic-Synthetic Integration Model: Solution to the Problem of Dualism and Secularism" in *Unio in Christo, 8 No. 2*. (Oct 2022), at ATLA: https://web.p.ebscohost.com/ehost/pdfviewer/pdfviewer.

Luno, Angel. *Etica*. (Florence: Le Monnier, 1992).

McGovern, Thomas. *What Christ Suffered*. (Huntington, Indiana: Our Sunday Visitor, 2020).

Metropolitan of Nafpaktos Hierotheos. *The Science of Spiritual Medicine: Orthodox Psychotherapy in Action*. (Levadia, Greece: Birth of Theotokos Monastery Pelagia, 2010).

Merriam-Webster's Online Dictionary. Truth. Archived 2009-12-29, at the Wayback Machine 2005, at https://www.merriam-webster.com/dictionary/truth.

Milton, Philip. "David Hume and the Eighteenth-Century Conception of Natural Law." *Legal Studies*, 2, no. 1 (1982): 14-33, at https://doi.org/10.1111/j.1748-121X.1982.tb00278.x.

Monod, Jacque. *Chance and Necessity: An Essay on the Natural Philosophy of Modern Biology.* Trans. A Wainhouse. (New York: Knopf, 1971).

Narayannan, Hari. "Freedom, Responsibility, and Jurisprudence." *Balkan Journal of Philosophy,* Vol. 10, Issue 1 (2018): 55, at CINAHL, https://web.p.ebscohost.com/ehost/pdfviewer/pdfviewer.

O'Keefe, Tim. "Ancient Theories of Freedom and Determinism," in The Stanford Encyclopedia of Philosophy. (Spring 2021 Edition), at https://plato.stanford.edu/archives/spr2021/entries/freedom-ancient/

"Online Etymology Dictionary at https://www.etymonline.com/ word/compassion.

"Oregon Death with Dignity Act 2022 Data Summary." (Oregon: Public Health Division, Center for Health Statistics, 8 March 2023), at https://www.oregon.gov/oha/PH/PROVIDERPARTNER-RESOURCES/EVALUATIONRESEARCH/DEATHWITHDIGNITYACT/Documents/year25.pdf.

Oxford Essential Quotations, 5 ed. (Oxford University Press, 2017), at https://www.oxfordreference.com/display/10.1093/acref/9780191843730.001.0001/q-oro-ed5-00007886.

Pope Francis. Declaration On Human Dignity *Dignitas Infinita*. (2 April 2024).

Saint Bridget. "Devotion to Our Lady of Sorrows," at https://carmelitesistersocd.com/devotion-to-our-lady-of-sorrows/.

Saint Francis DeSales. "Consoling Thoughts on Sickness and Death." Complied by Pere Huguet. (Charlotte, NC: TAN Books, 2013).

Sendrail, Marcel. *Historie Culturelle de la Maladie*. (Toulouse, 1980).

Sgreccia, Elio. *Personalist Bioethics: Foundations and Applications*. (Philadelphia, PA: The National Catholic Bioethics Center, 2012).

Sheen, Fulton. *The World's First Love*. (San Francisco, CA: Ignatius Press, 1996).

Tedeschi, Richard & Calhoun, Lawrence. *Trauma & Transformation: Growing in the Aftermath of Suffering*. (SAGE Publications, 1995).

Thrash, Todd, Laura Maruskin, Scott Cassidy, et. al. "Mediating Between the Muse and the Masses: Inspiration and the Actualization of Creative Ideas" in *Journal of Personality and Social Psychology, 98(3),* at https://doi.org/10.1037/ a0017907.

Turner, De Sales and Helen Cox. "Facilitating Post Traumatic Growth" in *Health Quality of Life Outcomes* Vol. 2, 34 (2004), at https://hqlo.biomedcentral.com/articles/10.1186/14777525-2-34#citeas.

Vansteenkiste, Maareten, Ryan Richard, & Bart Soenens. "Basic Psychological Need Theory: Advancements, Critical Themes, and Future Directions" in *Motivation and Emotion*, Vol. 44 (21 January 2020): 1-31, at https://doi.org/10.1007/s11031-019-09818-1.

von Speyr, Adrienee. *Handmaid of the Lord*. (San Fransisco, CA: Ignatius Press, 1985).

Van Zeller, Hubert. *The Mystery of Suffering.* (Notre Dame, IN: Christian Classics, 2015).

Watson, Richard. "René Descartes." Encyclopedia Britannica. (4 June 2024), at https://www.britannica.com/biography/Rene-Descartes.

Wawrytko, Sandra. "Aesthetics of Attentional Networks: Chinese Harmony and Greek Dualism" in *Journal of Chinese Philosophy, 47 No. 1(2),* (2020).

Waxman, Robert. "Five Philosophers on Free Will: Plato, Hobbes, Hume, Leibniz, and Hegel." (2019-03-29), at https://philarchive.org/rec/PHDFPO.

Weir, Ralph. *Christian Physicalism and the Biblical Argument for Dualism* in *International Journal for Philosophy of Religion No. 91 (2022),* at ALTLA: https://web.p.ebscohost.com/ehost/pdfviewer/pdfviewer?vid=0&sid=7a0573c7-51e3-4ac2-8441-31e4e36b71b3%40redis.

Wong, Paul, Richard Cowden, Claude Mayer, et al. "Shifting the Paradigm of Positive Psychology: Toward an Existential Positive Psychology of Wellbeing" in eds Andrew Kemp and Darren Edwards, *Broadening the Scope of Wellbeing Science: Multidisciplinary and Interdisciplinary Perspec-*

tives on Human Flourishing and Wellbeing. (London: Palgrave Macmillan, 2022).

Wong, Paul & Timothy Yu. "Existential Suffering in Palliative Care: An Existential Positive Psychology Perspective," in *Medicina* 57(9). (September 2021), at https://www.ncbi.nlm.nih.gov/ pmc/articles/PMC8471755/.

Wood, Richard. "In Defense of Dualism: Competing and Complementary Frameworks" in *Religious Studies and the Sociology of Religion in Critical Research on Religion, Vol. 4(3).* (SAGE, 2016), 292-298, at ATLA: https://web.p.ebscohost.com/ehost/viewarticle/render.

Wu, Yang, Lu Wang, Mengiun Tae, et al. "Changing Trends in the Global Burden of Mental Disorders from 1990 to 2019 and Predicted Levels in 25 Years" in *Epidemiology Psychiatry Science*, 32:e63. (7 November 2023), at https://www.ncbi.nlm.nih.gov/pmc/articles/ PMC10689059/.

Zaman, Rashid, Ahmed Hankir, Monem Jemni. "Lifestyle Factors and Mental Health" in *Psychiatry Danub 31 (Suppl 3).* Sep 2019, at https://pubmed.ncbi.nlm.nih.gov/31488729/.

www.ingramcontent.com/pod-product-compliance
Lightning Source LLC
Chambersburg PA
CBHW060838050426
42453CB00008B/736